Presented to _____

by _____

on _____

the growing reader Phonics Bible

written by
Joy MacKenzie

illustrated by
Jill Newton

TYNDALE KIDS

Tyndale House Publishers, Inc.
Wheaton, Illinois

Visit Tyndale's exciting Web site for kids at www.cool2read.com.
Also see the Web site for adults at www.tyndale.com.

Edited by Betty Free
Designed by Julie Chen

Published in association with the literary agency of Ann Spangler & Associates,
1420 Pontiac Road Southeast, Grand Rapids, MI 49506.

Library of Congress Cataloging-in-Publication Data
MacKenzie, Joy.
  The growing reader phonics Bible / Joy MacKenzie ; illustrated by Jill Newton.
    p. cm. — (The growing reader series)
Summary: Sixty-one Bible stories from the Old and New Testaments introduce phonetic sounds
from A to Z.
  ISBN 0-8423-3917-5 (hardcover) — ISBN 0-8423-6579-6 (CD)
  1. Readers—Bible. 2. Bible stories—Problems, exercises, etc. 3. Readers (Primary) [1. Readers.
2. Bible stories. 3. English language—Phonetics.] I. Newton, Jill, date. ill. II. Title.
  PE1127.B5 M33 2002
428.2—dc21   2001006434

Printed in Singapore
11 10 09 08 07 06 05 04
10   9   8   7   6   5   4   3

A children's Bible based on phonics! What a great idea! Wait!
Sixty-some stories . . . written in rhyme . . . filled with fun . . .
infused with phonics . . . fit for four-year-olds to eight-year-olds . . .
and ABSOLUTELY TRUE? You've got to be kidding! It can't be done.
Well, maybe . . . but not alone.

A WHOLEHEARTED THANK-YOU

. . . to my agent, Ann Spangler, whose brilliant
idea sparked this "impossible" undertaking

. . . to my husband, Bob MacKenzie, who cheered
my early efforts, thus fanning the "impossible"
into credible flame

. . . and to Betty Free, Julie Chen, Karen Watson, and
Linda Peterson Kenney, whose vigilance, inspiration, and
encouragement faithfully stoked the fire to full fruition.

No such endeavor is ever achieved by a single force. This
is the product of a working partnership between author,
agent, illustrator, editor, and all those other important
and wonderful people encompassed in the word *publisher*.
All of them in this case have created together in remark-
able unison—not just occasionally, I believe, with the
intervention of divine direction!

—JM

Contents

NEW TESTAMENT

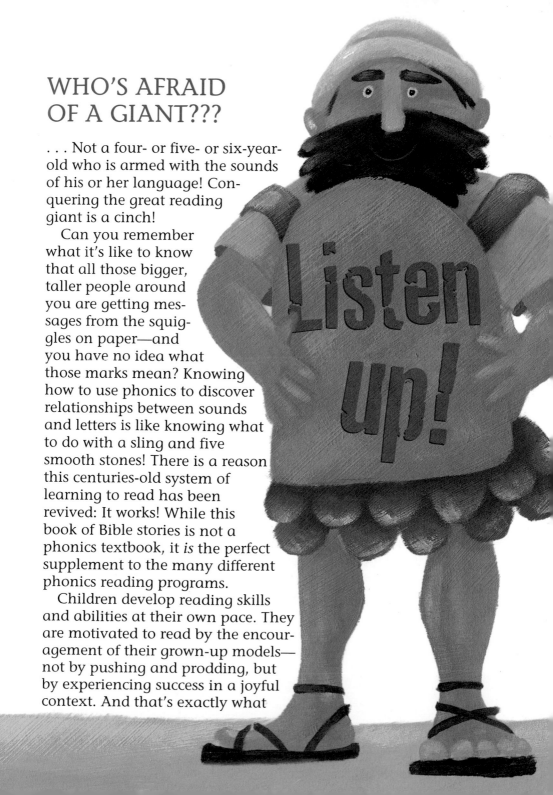

WHO'S AFRAID OF A GIANT???

. . . Not a four- or five- or six-year-old who is armed with the sounds of his or her language! Conquering the great reading giant is a cinch!

Can you remember what it's like to know that all those bigger, taller people around you are getting messages from the squiggles on paper—and you have no idea what those marks mean? Knowing how to use phonics to discover relationships between sounds and letters is like knowing what to do with a sling and five smooth stones! There is a reason this centuries-old system of learning to read has been revived: It works! While this book of Bible stories is not a phonics textbook, it *is* the perfect supplement to the many different phonics reading programs.

Children develop reading skills and abilities at their own pace. They are motivated to read by the encouragement of their grown-up models—not by pushing and prodding, but by experiencing success in a joyful context. And that's exactly what

The Growing Reader Phonics Bible provides for fledgling readers in its delightful rhymes, rhythms, sounds, and illustrations.

Beginning readers who aren't yet ready to read the stories themselves *are* ready to listen. In each story, they will delight in hearing a **star sound** of language and seeing it identified in **color**. Slowly and surely the relationship between the squiggly lines on a page and the sounds those squiggles stand for will begin to make sense.

Maturing readers will experience the joy of becoming more and more independent as relationships between sounds and letters leap into focus. This happens as they see the same **colored letters** repeated again and again in a story and as they engage in the fun of attacking and devouring words and ideas voraciously on their own.

All growing readers (including those already grown in age) will take delight in these stories, rich in sound and color, as well as in the imaginative illustrations that magnify the stories' meanings. Readers are bound to develop a natural curiosity about the words as well as the stories they tell.

Five smooth stones. Forty-four sounds. No armor needed!

One word of warning:
Prolonged contact with this book is likely to result in a life-long friendship with words—AND with the Word of God!

Boys and girls will meet God in these pages. They will develop a greater understanding of his love for them and his joy over them. And they will likely begin to claim the truth of God's Word for themselves. What better could we wish for the children we love?

May you and your growing readers find great delight in this book!

Joy MacKenzie

HEY, YOU!—YES, YOU . . .

To all the lively growing readers who will hear and read this book:

The stories in these pages
Are wonderful and true,
And filled with big surprises
That will astonish you!

An orphan girl who becomes a queen,
A giant who is a mean machine.
A chariot made of flaming fire,
A slithery snake who is a liar.
A storm stopped still by just three words,
And lunch served by a flock of birds.
A sea rolled back to make dry land,
And walls brought down by a marching band.
A shining star that helped to bring
Some wise men to a baby King!

These stories from the Bible
God wrote so you could see
How very much he loves you.
Look! Listen! Joyfully!

OLD TESTAMENT 🐝

A Grand Plan

Genesis 1:1-5

A long, long, long, long time ago, there was nothing.

Nothing.

Nothing at all.

There was no world.

There was no land.
No land. No sand.
No grass. No glass.
No ants. No plants.

There was nothing sad, nothing mad,
Nothing bad, nothing glad.
No caps or maps or naps.
No bats or cats or hats or rats.
And that is that.

Everything was black and dark. The dark was black as black can be. There was nothing but the blackness and water that was dark and deep. There was nothing at all but GOD.

God was there.

God had a plan.
He had a big plan.
A great big plan.
A great big, grand plan!

God said, "I will make a world! I will make a big, beautiful world." And God did. God made his big, beautiful world out of nothing.

He did not make it with a map.
He did not make it with a clap.
He did not make it with a zap.
He made it out of nothing at all.

God said words, and things began to happen. "Let there be light," he said. And there was light.

Light was here.
Light was there.
Light was everywhere.

The world was filled with light. And God said, "The light is good."

Then God saw that the dark was good too. And with the dark he made the first night!

With the light and the dark, God had made the first day!

Dark and light,
Day and night.

It was the first day **and** night EVER in our
world.

Words that tickle your tongue
Find these words in the story and say them again:
beautiful, clap, zap.

Guess What God Does Next!

Genesis 1:6-19

The world was new—just two days old.
What's next? Get ready! We are told
This was the day God made the sky
And set it in its place up high
Between the heavens and the seas.
Day three he made the fruits
*   and trees,*
And everywhere some
*   flowers he spread,*
All dressed in colors.
*   Then God said,*

"Day four I think that I will let
Them see my best idea yet!
By day the sun will shed its light.
I'll send the moon to shine at night.
The twinkle of the stars will tell
The world that everything is well."

Then God said, "It is good!"

Oh, yes! Oh, yes!

Yes, you CAN guess.

What God made next

Would be the best!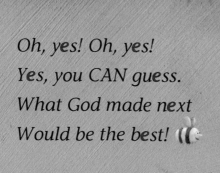

**Words that tickle
your tongue**
Find this word in the
story and say it again:
twinkle.

God Fills His Earth with Living Things

Genesis 1:1–2:3, 18-23

S—O—O—o—o—o—o . . .

Dark and light
And day and night,
Sky and seas
And land and trees,
Moon and sun
And stars were done.
But God's grand plan
Had just begun!

He filled his earth with living things
That move with fins
    and fly with wings!

Days five and six he must have
    had
Great fun. He said, "Now I will add
Birds with bills and fish
    with gills
And ants that sip up
    sticky spills . . .

"Some elephants with
    thick, gray skins
And hippos with big
    double chins.

14

"A piglet with a round, pink nose,
A yellow chick with orange toes.

"Lizards quick that flick their tails
And slugs with icky, sticky trails.

"A ladybug with wings and lots
Of itsy-bitsy polka dots."

"It's good, it's good," God said.
"It's good!"

If you will sit very still and read
carefully, you will learn about the next
amazing thing God did. Ready?

He said, "Just like myself I'll make
A man . . . and from his side I'll take
A rib to make a woman who
Will be his wife and helper, too."

So he made the very first Mr. and Mrs.
And they gave the very first
  hugs and kisses!

But wait! Did you hear?
Hold on a minute.
This is YOUR story!
You are in it!

It's the part of God's plan
Where people begin.

Yes, *this is* the place
Where YOU
    come in!

And God said,
"Oh, this is good—good,
good, GOOD!"

Then, on day seven, God
rested.

Words that tickle your tongue
Find these words in the story and say
them again: icky, sticky, itsy-bitsy.

S

A Sly Serpent Makes a Sad, Sorry Mess

Genesis 2:8-9, 15-17, 19-20; 3

"Mouse . . . moose . . .
Bear . . . bat . . .
Grasshopper . . . goose . . .
Cow . . . cat!"

That was the sound of Adam's voice. He was in the Garden of Eden, giving names to all the animals.

***"Sssssssssss** . . . So sweet . . .*
***Sssssssssss** . . . Taste and see*
How sweet is the fruit
Of that beautiful tree!"

That was the voice of the serpent in
the garden. He was telling Adam's wife,
Eve, to taste the fruit God said NOT to eat.

"I cannot. I will not!
Go, sly snake.
For God has said, 'NO!
This fruit do not take!'"

That was the voice of Eve. Eve wanted to
eat the fruit, but she also wanted to obey
God.

The snake laughed. "That's silly!
It's nice, and so yummy!
God wants you to taste it.
It's good for your tummy."

So Eve ate some fruit, and she gave
some to Adam. Adam liked the
fruit—it was gone in a second!

"Oh, Adam, dear Adam,
Let me see your face.
Let's go for a walk
In this beautiful place."

That was the voice of God. Every night he
came to the garden to walk and talk with Adam
and Eve.

But Adam and Eve
Had been bad, so they hid.
They were so very sad
About what they did.

And God was sad too,
So he sent them away
From his garden forever.
What a sad, sorry day!

That was the day when the world became
a sad, sorry mess for
a long, long time. And
all because . . .

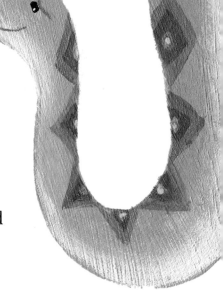

That serpent was bad,
That serpent was sly.
That serpent told Eve
A terrible lie!

And she believed it—Adam did
too.

Note: The letter **S** is not always in color in this
story. That's because it often makes a Z sound
instead of an **S** sound.

Words that tickle your tongue
Find these words in the story and say them again: mouse,
moose, grasshopper, goose.

More phonics fun
Read this story again to find every **c** that sounds like the **c** in
fa**c**e.

Brave, Bold Noah
Builds a Boat

Genesis 6:9–9:17

God's **b**ig, **b**eautiful world was full of people.
But most of the people did not love God.

*There were **b**ad people.*
There were mad people.
***B**ut not many glad people.*

Only one person was good. His name
was Noah.

"*Build a boat*," *said God.*
"*Right now! Right away!*"

Said Noah, "I will build it
Just as you say!"

"Ha! Ha!" The bad people laughed at Noah.

"*Noah is crazy!*
He's bonkers! Berserk!
He believes God told him
To do all this work!

"*There's no lake, no ocean,*
Not even a puddle!
Old Noah," *they said,*
"*Has his head in a muddle!*"

Brave, bold Noah went right on believing and building. *Bang!* went his hammer. *Buzzzzzz* went his saw.

Noah's
boat
got bigger
and bigger.

He was working on God's grand plan to get rid of all the **B**AD in his world.

When the **b**oat was **b**uilt, God said, "Good jo**b**, Noah!" Then God said,

"Now it's time to take your family—
You, your sons and wives;
Eight good men and women—
For I plan to save your lives.

"And take one pair
of every kind
Of animal—that's two!
*Get on the **b**oat. Get ready to float.*
And I'll take care of you."

So Noah and his wife, his three sons and their wives, and two of every animal God had made got on the **b**oat.

Bang! God shut the door.
And then . . .

It b**egan to rain! Oh, how
it rained. All the b**ottles and
b**owls and b**uckets and
b**athtub**s in the world
could not have held that
rain!

It rained . . . and rained . . . And
rained . . . and rained . . . and rained!

*Rain . . . rain . . . did NOT go away
For forty nights and forty days.
And nothing was left on the earth to see—
No laughing people, no house or tree.
Water was everywhere water could b**e.*

**Because Noah did what God told him to do,
His family was safe—and the animals, too!*

Many days later, when Noah looked out,
The world that he saw made him give a loud shout,
For God had taken the water away!
Noah called his family together to pray.
"We thank you, God, for keeping us dry!"
Then God put a rainbow in the blue sky.
And where the great flood of water had been,
God's beautiful world began growing again.

Words that tickle your tongue
Find these words in the story and say them again: bonkers, berserk.

God's Surprise Promise

Genesis 15:5; 17:17-19; 21:1-7

Twinkle, twinkle, stars so high,
***P**eeping at us from the sky.*
*Tiny **p**oints of s**p**arkling light*
***P**oking **p**inholes in the night.*

One thousand, two thousand,
Three thousand, four.
Five thousand, six thousand . . .
And many more.

God told his friend Abraham to count the
stars. But there were too many. Then God said,

"Guess what! Someday there will be as many people in your family as there are stars in the sky."

WOW!

That's more than all the . . .

Pickles and pears and peppers and peas
And all the filled pockets of pennies you please;

Peach pits and peanuts, pencils and pens,
Puddles, pins, pollywogs . . . where does it end?

Abraham was **perplexed!**

*He said, "That is a **puzzle!***
How can it be?
You have sent no children
To Sarah and me."

"Surprise! Surprise!
Oh, happy day!"
Said God. "Your son
Is on his way!"

Then God said, "You shall name him Isaac."

*Two parents so **proud***
*They were ready to **pop***
Cried, "Hooray! Our family
Will never stop!"

God's **pr**omise of a family with as many
people as the stars was sim**pl**y stu**p**endous!

Words that tickle your tongue
Find these words in the story and say them again: per**pl**exed,
stu**p**endous.

Good Job, God.
Thanks a Lot!

Genesis 24

One day Abraham called to his servant.

"Come, I have a job for you. My son, Isaac, needs a wife. But she cannot be from this town. You must find her in the town where I was born."

Off went the servant. He would not stop
Till his job was done for Isaac's pop.
He would look for a lady to be Isaac's wife—
Someone to love Isaac all of his life.

But how was the servant going to find
her? He knew he would need some help.

"So many women! This should be fun.
But how can I know which is the right one?"
He prayed to God, "Oh, help me see!
This job is far too big for me!"

So God put an idea in the servant's mind.
It was a wonderful idea!

"I've got it!" he hollered.
"That's it! Why not?
Good job, God.
Thanks a lot!

"When the girls of the town bring their pots
  to the well,
This is the way I'll be able to tell:
I will ask for a drink, and the young lady who
Says, 'I will get one for your camels too—'
She is the lady God knows is tops.
So when this happens, my job stops!"

And before the servant was done praying,
He heard a girl named Rebekah saying,
"I will get a drink for you,
And I will bring one for your camels, too!"

   The servant was very excited. Wow! How did
God do that?

The servant thanked God for helping him find
A top-notch lady—just the right kind
That Abraham wanted to be Isaac's wife,
To love him and help him the rest of his life!

Then the servant took Rebekah home
to Isaac. And Isaac loved Rebekah very much.
The two of them were happy to become
husband and wife.

Words that tickle your tongue
Find this word in the story and say it again: **top-no**tch.

Too Much of a Rush for Lunch

Genesis 25:19-34; 27:1-40

Esau and Jacob were twin brothers. But Esau was the son who was born first. So he got to have the birthright. This meant that after the boys grew **up**, Esau would take his father's place as the leader of the family.

Esau was always r**u**nning off to the woods to h**u**nt. Then he would come back home, where his brother, Jacob, liked to p**u**tter around the tent.

One day hungry Esau came home for lunch.
Jacob had made something yummy to munch.
"Oh, brother, I want some of that tasty meal."
"Okay," said Jacob, "then let's make a deal!

This mush for your birthright—that is the trade
I want for this yummy meal that I made."

"Well, I can't eat a birthright, so please fill my cup.
And be quick if you will. I'm starved. Hurry up!"

"Say for SURE," said Jacob, "what you want to do.
If you give up your birthright, then you're Number
   Two."

"Who cares about numbers? I'm in a bad mood.
You get the birthright, and I get the food!"

So Jacob gave his brother a full cup of yummy
mush, and Esau ate until he was stuffed.

Much later, when their father, Isaac, got old,
he blessed Jacob. And Jacob became the leader
of the family. Then Esau was very upset, and he
didn't feel much love for Jacob, his brother.

Esau was sorry he had been in such a rush for lunch. He had given up everything—just for a cup of mush!

Words that tickle your tongue
Find these words in the story and say them again: yummy mush.

More phonics fun
Read this story again to find every **o** that sounds like the **o** in son.

Hate Can't Wait

Genesis 37

Joseph had eleven brothers. Ten were older and one was younger. But Joseph was his father's favorite. This made his big brothers angry.

Joseph told his family about a dream. The story of his dream made his family think they would all have to kneel down in front of Joseph someday. This also made his big brothers angry.

They said that they would find a way to get rid of Joseph!

"This goody-good brother, we all love to hate—
Dad likes him best, so we just cannot wait.
Let us get rid of him. He cannot stay.
Shall we just kill him or give him away?"

Well, Joseph came over the very next day
To the place where they worked but did not hear
    them say:
"Here comes that dreamer we are to obey.
Let's get him! Oh, this will be our lucky day!"

The brothers ganged up on Joseph and ripped off his nice coat. They hated Joseph because of his coat—it was a special gift from Father. So they threw Joseph down into a big hole in the ground. They were going to kill him. Then they saw some traders from Egypt.

Joseph's older brothers sold him to the traders to be a slave. "We will shake dirt and blood on the beautiful coat that Father made for him," they said. "When we take it home, maybe Father will think a wild animal ate him!"

Those lamebrains cried,
  "Yay!
We are rid of that pest!"
But what happened next,
They could never have
  guessed.

Joseph did not go to Egypt alone. God went straight to Egypt with him! 🐝

Words that tickle your tongue
Find this word in the story and say it again: lamebrains.

More phonics fun
Read this story again to find every **e** that sounds like the **e** in th**ey**.

Egypt's Happy Dream Team

Genesis 39:1–41:44

God took good care of Joseph in Egypt. The king had an important helper who said, "Joseph, you shall be the keeper of my house!" But the mean lady of the house said something about Joseph that wasn't true. Her husband believed her evil words, and Joseph ended up in jail!

Jail was not a nice place to be.
Joseph was put in a room for three.
It was dark and scary with things that creep—
A very hard place to get any sleep.

The other two men told what they had seen
In their dreams and asked Joseph, "What does this
  mean?"

59

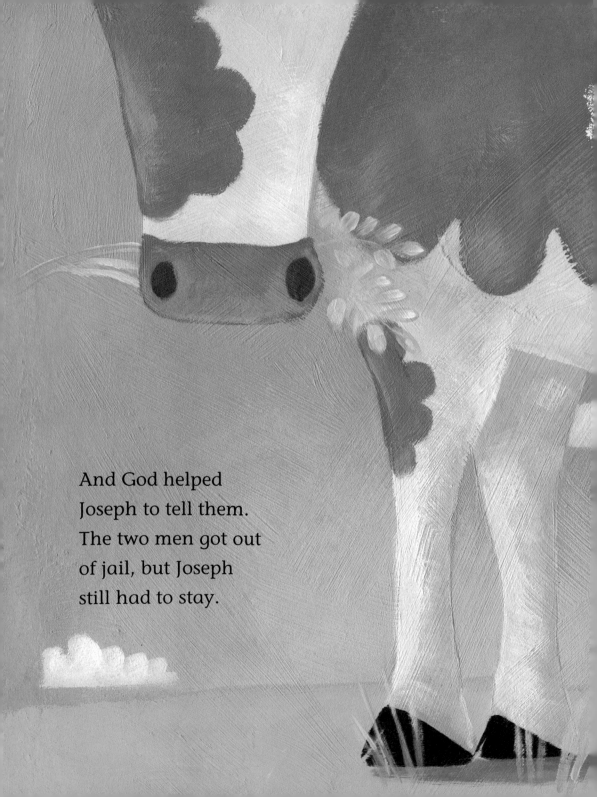

And God helped
Joseph to tell them.
The two men got out
of jail, but Joseph
still had to stay.

Now the king had a
dream about cows
and wheat.

So Joseph was called to sit at his feet
And tell of the dream: "For seven long years
We all can eat well without any fears.
But the next seven years will not be so sweet.
For God will bring famine, with no food to eat!"

"Eek!" yelled the king. "Just what will we do?"
"Listen," said Joseph, "to God's plan for you.
The years we have plenty, choose someone to lead
The people to save up the food we will need.
In the lean years of famine, our barns full of wheat
Will give all of Egypt plenty to eat!"

"A very good plan—I want you to lead us.
Your God," said the king, "is the one who will feed
   us!"

The king was happy with Joseph. He gave
Joseph his ring, new clothes to wear, a chariot
to ride in, and lots of men to help him.
Everyone in Egypt would kneel before Joseph
when he rode by in his chariot!

The king was pleased to tell Joseph that he was now the second most important leader in Egypt. Only the king himself was more important.

Words that tickle your tongue
Find this word in the story and say it again: chariot.

More phonics fun
Read this story again to find every **i** as in chariot, every **ie** as in bel**ie**ve, and every **y** as in bab**y**.

Wise Joseph Frightens His Brothers, Then Invites Them to Lunch! Why?

Genesis 42–45

Egypt and all the lands around it had seven good years with plenty to eat. Then the famine came. The land was dry. And soon there was no food to buy in the land where Joseph's family lived. The people were hungry. The children were crying for food.

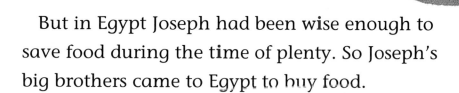

But in Egypt Joseph had been wise enough to save food during the time of plenty. So Joseph's big brothers came to Egypt to buy food.

When ten brothers came to kneel at his feet,
Joseph could not believe the surprise.
He knew them, but they did not guess who HE was.
So he said, "Take a hike—you are spies!"

"Oh no!" they cried. "We are here to buy food.
We are brothers—ten here, one home, and one
   dead."
"Well, if it is true, bring the little one here.
But if you are lying, **I** WILL have your head!"

Joseph threw his brothers in jail for three days.
Then he said to his men, "Fill their bags with
wheat. And in their bags, hide the money they
gave us."

When he let the brothers go, Joseph kept one
in jail and sent the others on their way. He
knew his big brothers would come back from
home with Benjamin, the little brother he loved
so much.

On the way home, one
brother found money in
his bag. All of the
brothers were afraid
when they saw the money.

Oh what a sight
To watch their fright
And hear their sighs.
They remembered the lies
To their father and they
Said, "Now we will pay
For the terrible day
We sold Joseph away!"

When Jacob, the father, heard the story, he
was afraid too. He said that he might never see
his youngest son, Benjamin, again if he let him
go to Egypt. But with no food to eat, everyone
would die.

Jacob did not want to lose the lives of all his sons, so he let Benjamin go to Egypt.

Back to Egypt the brothers
   hiked.
Joseph was delighted
To see little Ben and said to
   his brothers,
"Welcome!" and invited
The bunch for lunch with
   Simeon,
The brother who had stayed.
Then Joseph put in their bags
   of wheat
The money they had paid.

One last time he wanted to test
The older brothers' pride.
He told a helper, "In Benjie's bag
My silver cup you must hide."

As soon as there was morning light,
The brothers said good-bye.
They started out for home again.
Then Joseph's man did fly
Right after them to check their bags
And see who stole the cup.
Surprise! In little brother's bag,
The silver did turn up!

Yikes! The one who had the cup
Would be the ruler's slave.
Leaving Ben behind would send
Their father to his grave.

Back at Joseph's house, the older brothers all
fell down in fright to beg for the life of their
little brother.

Judah cried, "Hey, I will stay.
I know you are the boss.
Please let Ben go or Dad will die.
He cannot take such loss!"

Then Joseph could not hide his feelings any
longer.

"I'm Joseph, the one whom you sold long ago,
But now I'm the king's advisor. And so,
Because I can see you've become good and kind,
I want you to hurry back home and find
Our father and bring him back here—we'll be fine.
We'll all live together in this land of mine."

Joseph burst into tears and opened his arms
wide to hug his brothers.

Then the brothers left right away again. They went home to tell their father, Jacob, the good news. They went to bring him back to his son Joseph. They told Jacob he could live in Egypt with all twelve sons and their families.

Oh my!
Don't cry.
Smile
A while!

The people in Jacob's family are happy again. It's a very nice ending for a wild and weepy story!

Words that tickle your tongue
Find these words in the story and say them again: delighted, yikes.

More phonics fun
Read this story again to find every y that sounds like the y in cry and buy.

A Boat for Baby Moses

Exodus 1:8–2:10

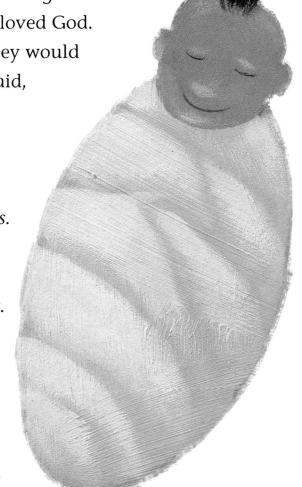

In Egypt there was a new king. He did
not like the people who loved God.
Oh no! He was afraid they would
take over his land. He said,

"I know how to fix this.
We won't let God's people
  grow.
We will kill their baby boys.
Then they all will know
Who is boss, and the loss
Will wipe their leaders out.
No more men like Joseph,
  please.
I will send a scout . . .

75

To visit every Hebrew home.
We'll go to every mother
And take away her sons this day—
Yes, every baby brother!"

Oh, what a sad, sorry day. Little Miriam was so afraid. Three months ago, her mother had given birth to a baby boy. Now the baby was growing too big and too old to hide in the house. Miriam was afraid the king's men would find her baby brother.

But God gave the baby's mother a bold idea. She made a cradle of weeds. She made it light and tight so it would float on water. Then she put the baby in the little boat and set it to float on a river.

Miriam stayed close by. As she watched over her brother, she might have hummed a little tune like this:

Little brother in a boat,
God and I will watch you float.
While the river breezes blow,
Rest well in your basket low.

One day, as Miriam was watching her brother, the daughter of the king came to the river with her maids. The princess spied the little floating basket. When she opened the cover, the baby began to cry.

"This must be a Hebrew child," said the princess. Slowly she took the baby out of the basket to hold him close.

At that moment, Miriam came out from her hiding place. She spoke to the princess. "May I go to find a nurse for the baby?"

"Oh yes, please do!" the princess said.
Miriam was excited.
And when she brought her mother back,
The princess was delighted.

She said, "If you will nurse the babe
As if he were your own,
   Then I will pay you well." Of course,
The princess couldn't have known
The woman who was going to help
   WAS the baby's mother!
            No way could she
            have guessed
            God's plan
            For Miriam's
            baby brother.

         The baby's
         mother took him
         home. When he
         was older, his mother
         took him to the
         princess. "I will
         call him Moses,"
         the princess said.

So Moses grew up in the palace—the home of the king. The princess loved him as her **own** son. God smiled. He had big plans for Moses. Big, grand plans! 🐝

Words that tickle your tongue
Find this word in the story and say it again: princess.

A Huge Job for Moses: Will He Refuse?

Exodus 2:23–4:20

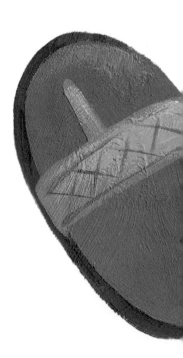

Right in front of Moses' eyes, a bush was on fire. But it was not burning up! Moses was confused. He ran to look.

But then he heard the voice of God. "Not too close, Moses. Take off your shoes. For you are standing on holy ground."

Well, when God speaks, you DO NOT refuse.
You usually want to hear his views!

Moses did not argue. He had his shoes off in a few seconds. "Moses," said God, "I have a huge job for you. You must go back to Egypt and bring my people out."

Moses was mute. His tongue would not work.
He stuttered and sputtered. He felt like a jerk.
He fussed and he fumed.
He wasn't amused.
He stammered, "I'm not . . .
not the best man to use.

I want to do anything that you
may ask.
But I'm only human. I CAN'T
DO THIS TASK!"

"I will help you. Just tell the people that I am the true God and I have sent you."

"Are you sure, God? Don't you know I am not very smart? What if your people don't believe me?"

"What is that
in your hand?"
asked God.

"A stick," said Moses.

"Throw it down," said God. Moses did it right
on cue.

SHAZAMM! The stick became a snake,
And Moses did a double take!

"Now pick it up by the tail," said God. So
Moses picked up the huge snake.

Before that snake could give Moses a lick,
SHAZAMM! again—it became a stick!

Then God told Moses to cover his hand. When
Moses looked at it again, this is what he saw:

Nasty sores were itching and oozing.
Moses could tell that he was losing!

"Look again!" said God, and the sores
went POOF!

"Now do you need some better proof?"

"Whew! You're quick! What a cure!
I know your plan is good and pure.
And God, your Word should be my cue.
But can't you see my point of view?

—I'M STILL NOT GOOD
AT TALKING TO PEOPLE!"

"Okay," said God. "Then your brother, Aaron,
can go along with you. He speaks well.

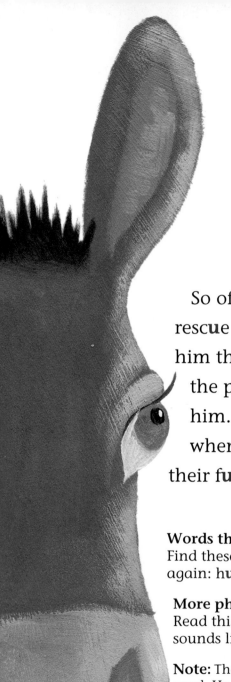

"Now don't just stand there, stubborn as a m**u**le. Stop f**u**ming and get going."

*"Move it! Do what I ask y**o**u to. Wherever y**o**u are, I will be with y**o**u!"*

So off Moses went to Egypt to rescue God's people. He took with him the stick he would **u**se to show the people that God really sent him. Then they couldn't arg**u**e when he told them God's plan for their f**u**ture.

Words that tickle your tongue
Find these words in the story and say them again: h**u**ge, arg**u**e, f**u**ming.

More phonics fun
Read this story again to find every **ew** that sounds like the **ew** in f**ew**.

Note: The word "you" is often taught as a sight word. However, the letter **U** in each "y**o**u" in this story is in color because the *sound* is a long **U** sound.

I've Had It! Just Scram! Get Out of This Land!

Exodus 7–12

"Let God's people go," said Moses.

"No!" said the king.

"Yes!" said Moses.

"No!" said the king. "No! No! No!"

*The king was **as** stubborn **as** ten packs*
of mules.
And he wanted nothing to do with
God's rules.
*He wanted God's people to work **as** his*
slaves.
*He would keep them **u**ntil they fell*
into their graves.

89

"Get to work!" yelled the king.
"Don't stop for a thing!
No stopping, no dropping,
No flopping! Get hopping!"
They worked in the sun—
But it wasn't much fun.

And the king kept yelling,
"Just work, work, work!"
That terrible king
Was a jerk, jerk, jerk!

No matter what Moses said, the king would not listen. So God began another grand plan. He made all kinds of bad things happen to the people of Egypt.

Blood in the water,
  killing their fishes.

Frogs jumping into
   their cereal dishes.

Lice in their hair,
   little flies that would bite.
Cattle just dropping down
   dead in the night.

Boils on the people and hail on their heads.
Locusts that eat all their fine flowerbeds.
Darkness—three days without one bit of light.
And then God sent death to each house one night.

Finally the Egyptian people cried so loudly
that the king got up in the middle of the night
and called Moses and Aaron to his house.

In a burst of anger the king yelled, "Go!
Just go," he hollered. "Yes, go! Go! GO!

I've had it! Your God
has made himself
clear.
Take your people and
scram—get out of
here!"

And WOW!
Did they go!

Words that tickle your tongue
Find these words in the
story and say them again:
scram, stubborn.

A Dry Road across the Bottom of the Sea

Exodus 12–14

God's people could not wait to get out of Egypt.
They had been slaves to the cruel king for a
long time.

The people were quick to pack up that day
When God sent them clouds to show them the way:
A white cloud to lead them when it was light,
A bright cloud of fire to lead them at night.

God led his people to a place by the Red Sea,
but almost as soon as they got there, the cruel
king wished he had not let them go. So he sent
his great army to go after them in fast chariots.

When the people saw the Egyptians coming, they were so afraid they were ready to puke. They fussed and they fumed until they were blue in the face. "Where is God now?" they wondered.

"We have followed all his clouds and his routes.
And here we are, trapped with no swimming suits.
We try to obey each of his wishes.
But we are just humans—not tuna fishes!

"We will NEVER get across this sea," they moaned. "We are all going to DIE!"

"HEY YOU WITH THE BAD ATTITUDE!" cried Moses. "COOL IT!" He was trying to quiet the people.

"Never mind chariots, armies, and kings.
God can do STUPENDOUS things!
You will not believe what God will do.
Just wait till you see what he's planned for you!"

The king's army was due there at almost any moment. So Moses touched the waters of the Red Sea with his stick. And the waters opened like a gate to make a dry road across the bottom of the sea.

On cue, the water rolled back
    like a wall.
And the people did not get wet
    at all!

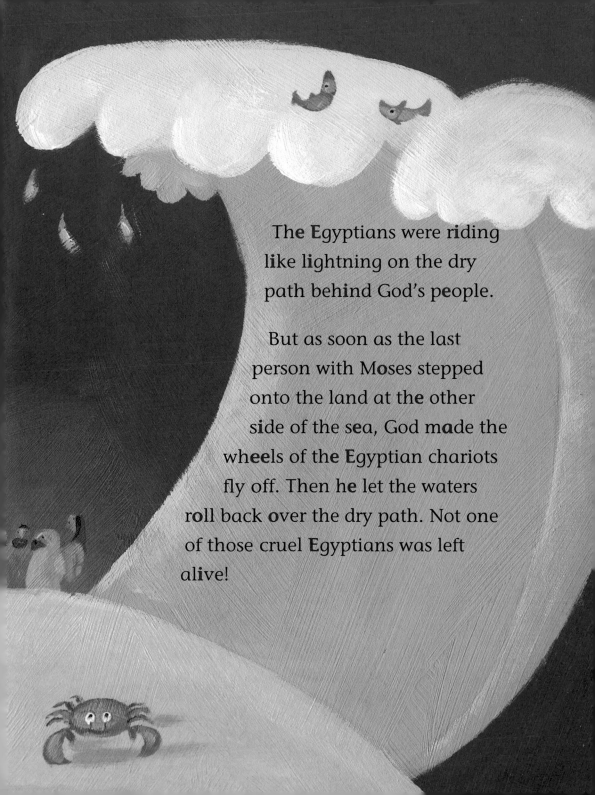

The Egyptians were riding
like lightning on the dry
path behind God's people.

But as soon as the last
person with Moses stepped
onto the land at the other
side of the sea, God made the
wheels of the Egyptian chariots
fly off. Then he let the waters
roll back over the dry path. Not one
of those cruel Egyptians was left
alive!

Hooray for God! He did a STUPENDOUS thing!

Safe on the land, God's people were singing
Praises to God for his help in bringing
Them out of a land of hurt and hard work,
Away from the king who was such a big jerk!

Words that tickle your tongue
Find these words in the story and say them again:
jerk, lightning.

More phonics fun
Read this story again and find every e as in they, every i as in chariot, and every y as in dry.

Meat and Manna
from Heaven

Exodus 14:21-22; 16:1–17:7

God had done the impossible. He had saved his people from the Egyptians by moving the waters of the Red Sea.

But now God's people had to walk across a huge, dry desert. They were tired and hungry. And they were mad at God and Moses.

Mumble, grumble,
Gripe, and groan;
Mutter, sputter,
Murmur, and moan.

101

The people acted like bad children. They said God had left them to die. But God heard them, and one more time, he did the impossible.

Yes, God heard all of their mumbling words.
Each evening he sent big clouds of birds.
The people said, "Here comes supper—look!
Our God has sent us some meat to cook!"

Every morning as the sun rose high,
Some manna bread fell down from the sky!
With morning manna and birds for meat,
Tummies were full of good things to eat.

As they **m**ade the long walk
across the wide desert, they ca**m**e to
a place where there was no water.
They were tired. Their **m**ouths were dry.
So they got **m**ad at Moses and God
again.

*Mum*ble, gru*mb*le,
Gripe, and groan;
*M*utter, sputter,
*M*urm*u*r, and **m**oan.

So what did God do? He told Moses to hit a rock with his stick. Moses did as God said, and . . .

Out of that rock came—what do you think?
Much more water than they could drink!

God had done the impossible—again. God ALWAYS takes care of his children!

Words that tickle your tongue
Find these words in the story and say them again:
impossible, mumbling.

ATTENTION! God Has Something to Say!

Exodus 19:16–20:21; 31:18–32:15-19, 30-34; 34:1-11

One day Moses and the rest of God's people were camping near a big mountain.

Rrrr-umble. Rrrr-umble.
Crrr . . . aaack! Bang! BOOM!
Rrrr-umble. Rrrr-umble.
Zzzz . . . aaap! BAZOOM!

What thunder! What lightning!
What a loud noise!
"Fear not," said Moses.
"It is God's voice!
He wants your attention.
Hear ALL he will say."

"God is too loud,"
Thought the people. "No way!"
They ran to their tents,
All shaking with fear.
"Have God tell YOU
What he wants us to hear!"

So God told Moses to come up on the mountain to listen for the people. God said he would give Moses some rules. God knew that his people would need these rules to have happy lives.

To help them remember, God made a list of ten good rules. They go like this:

1. Do not EVER worship any other God but me.
2. Do NOT make gods of statues or of pictures that you see.
3. Please say my name with love—never in a bad way.

4. Work HARD six days,
   but on day SEVEN, rest and pray.
   Save that day for worship.
   Make your busy week stop.

5. If you want a good, long life,
   then honor Mom and Pop!

6. *Never, **never**, NEVER take another person's life.*

7. *Do NOT mess around with another man's wife.*

8. *Never steal.*

9. *Never lie.*

10. *Don't wish with all your might*
    To have what someone else has—
    Now do what is right!

These rules were important.
These rules were for good.
Anyone who obeyed
These important rules would
Live a life that was blessed.
But people are known
To forget about rules,
So God carved them in
    stone.

Moses was up on the mountain with God for a long time. The people began to think he would never come back again. So they made a god of their own out of gold. And they danced and sang and had a wild party.

Uh-oh! Suddenly the people looked up to see someone coming down the mountain. It was Moses. And he was angry.

When he saw the people running wild, Moses threw down the stones on which God had written his good rules. And the stones were broken to pieces. Then Moses had a long talk with the people about their sinful ways.

The **next day Moses went
back up the **mountain** to ask
God to forgive his people, and
God wrote his important rules
o**n two new stones. God made
a cove**n**ant with Moses—a **new
promise that he would take care
of **a**ny**on**e who obeyed his ten
important rules.

And God always keeps his cove**n**ant.

Words that tickle your tongue
Find these words in the story and say them again: bazoom,
thunder, lightning, covenant.

Giant Jericho Tumbles Down

Joshua 6

God's people had been walking across the desert for forty long years. At last they came near the wonderful land God had promised them. All they had to do was cross the Jordan River and they would be in the new land.

Their leader, Moses, had died. Before he died, Moses had told the people that Joshua would be their new leader.

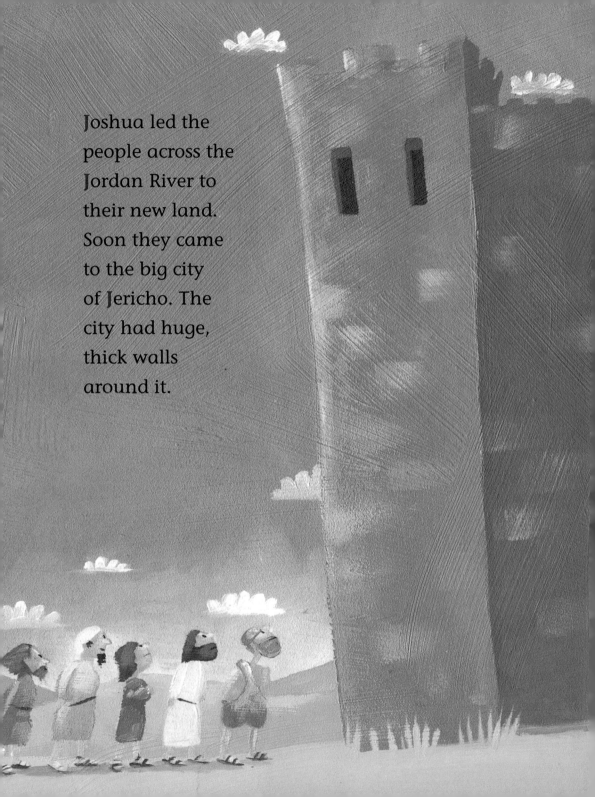

Joshua led the people across the Jordan River to their new land. Soon they came to the big city of Jericho. The city had huge, thick walls around it.

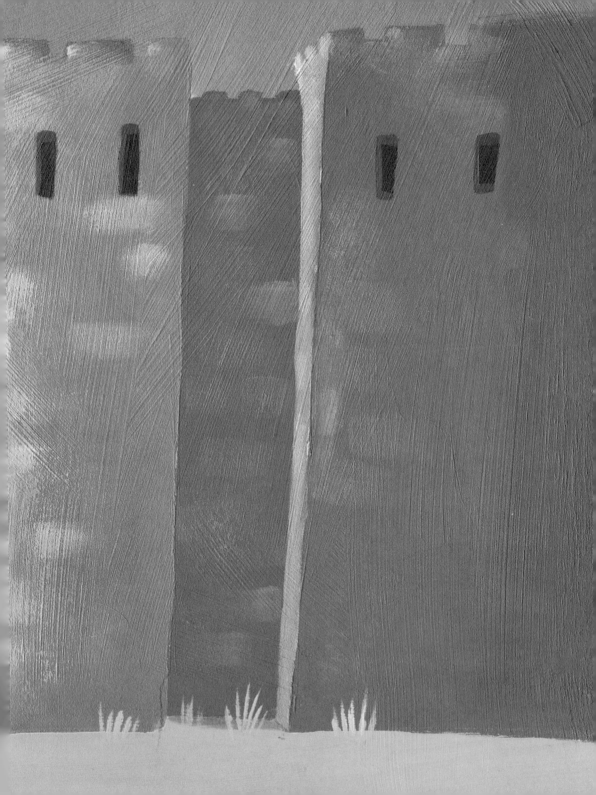

And the people
who lived in Jericho
did not want God's
people to come in.

Joshua said to the
people, "Let's go!
God's plan is for
us to have Jericho."

"Our leader is joking,"
they thought. "Hasn't he
Looked up at these
jumbo-size walls
that we see?

His brain must be jelly.
No way can we win.
The giants in Jericho
won't let us in!"
"Now listen!" said Joshua.
"God has his ways.
Can you keep a secret
for seven long days?
God's plan is as simple
as playing with toys.
We'll take this huge city
by just making noise!
I know it sounds crazy.
But like it or not,
His plan is the only one
we have got!"

Then Joshua told the people the secret of God's message. "We must march around the walls of Jericho one time each day for six days. Some of our people who have horns will blow them as we march. But do not talk. Don't say a word until I tell you to shout.

"On day seven we must march around the walls seven times. Then there will be a big surprise. You will not believe it. Your eyes will bulge right out of your head!"

"This is just too strange,"
Said the people. "Can we do it?"
"Come on!" hollered Joshua.
"Let's get to it!"

So once a day for six days the horn blowers blew and everyone marched. On day seven all the people joined together again. They made seven trips around the gigantic walls. Then Joshua said to the horn blowers,

*"Blow as loud as you can—you must blow your
    horns out.*
And the rest of you people, give one giant shout!"
*So they blew and they shouted, and the walls of that
    town*
Came crumbling, jumbling, tumbling down!

Joshua had believed God's strange message. And the people had joined together to obey God's plan. Now they could all enjoy the land God had promised them.

Words that tickle your tongue
Find these words in the story and say them again: bulge, gigantic, jumbo-size.

More phonics fun
Read this story again and find every g that sounds like the g in giant, page, and judge.

An All-Wrong Story Ends Up Right

The book of **R**uth

This story starts with news that's bad
And makes you want to cry.
Naomi has a husband and
Two sons. Then all three die.

Everything was sad and wrong. Naomi wanted to move back to the land where she grew up. Then one son's wife, **R**uth, talked to Naomi.

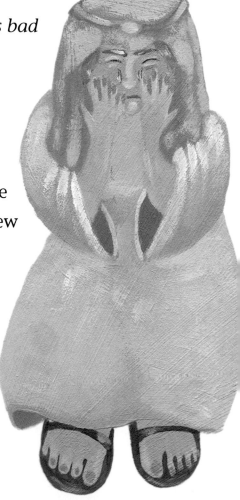

"I'll love you and will stay with you.
And I want you to know
That wherever you would like to move,
That's where I want to go."

"Oh no, my dear, I'm old, I fear.
And you are young and fair."
"Then we will need each other," said Ruth.
"We will be a pair!"

Naomi and Ruth started out together to make a new home. There had been years of famine in the land where Naomi grew up. So it was hard to find food. There was no one to care for the two women. So every day Ruth ran to a farm to gather scraps of barley grain that were left in the field.

A rich man named Boaz was the owner of the farm. Each morning Boaz would watch Ruth as she worked hard to gather the grain for herself and Naomi.

It pleased him that **Ruth** took such good care of
her mother-in-law. Soon something wonderful
began to happen.

*Whenever Boaz looked at **Ruth**,*
His heart went pitty-pat.

It wasn't long before he knew
That he had fallen flat
In love with this fine lady.
So he asked if she would be
His wife. She said, "My heart,
I fear, will jump right out of me.
I'm so happy. Yes! Oh yes!
I will be your bride."
When Naomi heard the happy news,
She hugged their necks and cried.

So Ruth and Boaz were married, and soon Naomi had a baby grandson to hold in her arms.

The four of them had a wonderful life.
Boaz was proud to have Ruth as his wife.
But maybe the best part—the fun of it—
Was when Grandmother came to baby-sit!

Words that tickle your tongue
Find these words in the story and say them again: pitty-pat, grandmother.

Samuel, Child Called by God

1 Samuel 1–3

Hannah had a good husband and a good home. But Hannah **did** not have a child. That made her sad deep down in her heart.

*So Hannah went to worship one **day**.*
She bowed her head and began to pray.
"Oh, God, please send me a baby
*   boy*
To make my sad heart glad
*   with joy.*
When he is older, I'll give
*   him to you*
To help at your tent-house.
*   That's what I'll **do**."*

Eli was the leader of the tabernacle, the tent-house where people worshiped God. Eli heard Hannah's prayer. He said to Hannah, "May God give you your wish."

To Hannah's delight, she soon had a child. And she named him Samuel.

Hannah loved little Sam the way mothers do.
She held him and hugged him and prayed for him
  too—
That he would grow up to know of God's ways,
To love God and serve God all of his days.

Then, not forgetting her promise to God, Hannah took her son to the tabernacle to help Eli.

Now Eli had two sons of his own. But those boys were bad. They did not want to serve God or their father. So Eli was happy to have Samuel for his helper. He cared for Samuel and taught him to obey God's Word.

Samuel was glad to serve
Eli. And he liked it
when his
mom and
dad came
to visit.

Then one night the most astounding thing happened to Samuel!

He was sound asleep when someone called, "Sam!"
He sat up and listened. He said, "Here I am."

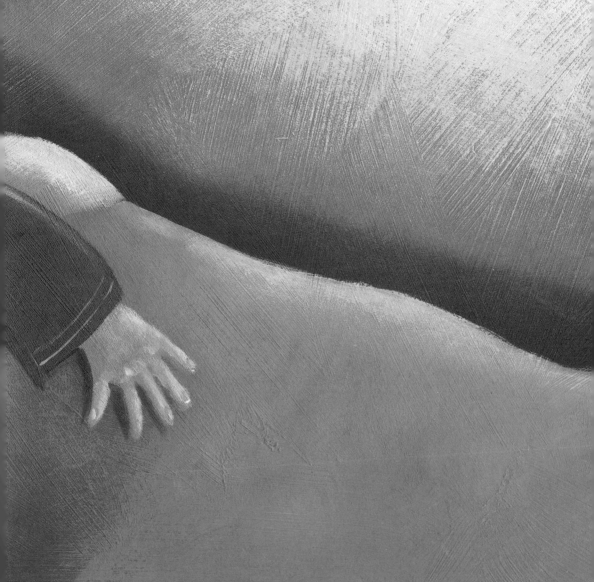

Then he ran to find Eli, but old Eli said,
"I **did** not call you. Now go back
    to be**d**."

Soon he hear**d** someone call "Samuel"
    again.
Eli said, "You must be **d**reaming!" But then,
A thir**d** time he hear**d** his name. How very o**dd**!
Then Eli was sure the voice calling was Go**d**.

So back to be**d** Sam went to listen once more.
Was Go**d** really calling to him? An**d** what for?
He lay wi**d**e awake in the **d**ark. Then that same
Kin**d** voice he ha**d** heard once again calle**d** his
    name.
An**d** this time Sam answere**d**, "Lor**d**, it is clear
That you want to talk. I am rea**d**y to hear."

Then God spoke these wor**d**s to Samuel:

"The sons of Eli are wicked men.
You must tell Eli that I will not let his
family keep working for me. They cannot serve
in my tabernacle."

The next morning Samuel was afraid. But he did not hide God's message from Eli.

The news made Eli sad, but he understood. "It is the word of the Lord," he said. "Let him do what is good and right."

Words that tickle your tongue
Find these words in the story and say them again: tabernacle, astounding.

A Small Shepherd—
Israel's Next Ruler

1 Samuel 16:1-13

The boy Samuel grew up to be a man of God
and a ruler in Israel. The king of Israel was a
man named Saul. King Saul was a sinful man.
He did not listen to God.

So the Lord said to Samuel, "It is time for
Israel to look for a new king. Fill your
horn with oil and get ready."

A new king should not have been so hard to find,
For Israel had lots of strong men, but God's mind
Was made up already. He said, "I'll choose from
The children of Jesse. Now tell him to come
And bring all his sons, so that we all can see
Just which of those brothers the new king will be."

Seven boys who were strong and good-looking
   and tall
Came to Samuel, who gave a welcome to all.
But Samuel said, "Jesse, did you not bring
Every one of your children? The one to be king
Does not seem to be here. These boys are smart
And handsome and strong, but God knows the
   heart."

"I have one little fellow who tends to the sheep."

"Then send for him. I have a promise to keep.
I will bless with this oil only one boy's head—
The boy God has chosen. I'll do as God said."

That is why **little** David was **led** to this place.

And the spirit of God could be seen on his face.

When Samue**l** anointed this smal**l** shepherd son

To be Israe**l**'s king, the choosing was done! 🐝

Words that tickle your tongue
Find these words in the story and say them again: oil, anointed.

Good-bye, Goliath!

1 Samuel 17

Who was afraid of a giant? The whole army of Israel—that's who!

For forty days **G**oliath, the Philistine **g**iant, stood on a hill. He stood there morning and night, yelling at King Saul's army in a **g**reat, **g**ruff voice.

"I will fight for the Philistines," he **g**rowled. "Who will fight for Israel?"

*This giant was **g**argantuan—*
*That's bi**gg**er than bi**g** can be!*
*He must have **g**obbled mounds of food*
*And **g**uzzled half the sea.*

143

He wore a heavy suit of armor
And carried an iron sword.
His loud and grumpy grumblings could
No longer be ignored.

   Not far away, in Israel's army camp, King Saul was looking for someone to fight Goliath. Soon he saw David, the shepherd boy, coming to bring bread and grain and cheese to his brothers who were in Saul's army.

   When David heard Goliath's loud bragging, he went to King Saul.

"This guy is evil, and he should be dead.
So I will fight him and win," David said.
"That isn't possible," said King Saul,
"You are a child, and he's nine feet tall!"

"The lions and bears that have grabbed my sheep,
I have killed with my hands. And Israel won't sleep
Till we get this old goat who laughs at our fear."

"If you MUST go," said Saul, "please take my gear.
You can put on my helmet, armor, and sword."

"Good grief!" giggled
David. "It's stiff as a board!
I can't fight like this.
I'll just wear my
own skin."

He turned toward
Goliath and said
with a grin,
"A God who can help
me kill lions and
bears
Is as good and as
great with giant
affairs!"

Then David dug out of
his pocket his sling made
of leather and sticks. He
jogged down to the creek

and gathered five smooth stones. He put them in his bag and went out to greet Goliath.

David gazed up into the sky and grinned. "Okay, God. Let's go get this gigantic gummy bear!"

When Goliath saw David coming to meet him, that great giant got angry. "Do you think I am a dog?" he growled. "Why do you come against me with sticks?"

David gave Goliath this answer: "You come to me with sword and spear. But I come to you in the name of God. Soon the whole world will know that there is a God in Israel."

Then David put one little stone
in his sling.
And he swung it around, and he
slung the thing.

The great giant fell with his
face to the ground
And lay still as rock—a
gargantuan mound!

When David's small stone hit Goliath's big head,
Little David had won. The giant was dead!

Words that tickle your tongue
Find these words in the story and say them again:
gargantuan, good grief.

Jonathan, a Best Friend for David

1 Samuel 17:51–20:42

Hurrah! Hurrah! Goliath was dead.
David had cut off the giant's head!
The rest of the Philistines ran away.
Saul's armies cried, "What a happy day!"

David had won the hearts of all of Israel's people. Saul honored David and invited him to live in the palace. There David met Jonathan, Saul's son, and the boys became best friends.

King Saul could hear the oohs and aahs
Of people when they talked
About this brave, young shepherd boy.
And everywhere Saul walked,

151

David was the people's hero.
This was NOT a good thing—
That people might love David more
Than they loved Saul, the king!

Saul became annoyed. He thought to himself, "This young boy is getting more attention than I am!"

Then one day, as David was playing the harp for him, Saul got so upset thinking about the people's love for David that he threw his spear across the room at David. Then David became afraid of Saul and ran away.

Jonathan was amazed and alarmed at his father's anger. He said, "Papa, David has done great things for you and for Israel. Why would you want to harm him?"

Jonathan and David
were such good friends
that they did not like
to be apart.

So Jon got his father, the king, to **a**gree that if David would come back, the king would not start any more trouble.

But King Saul w**a**s so jealous that he could not keep his **a**greement. Once **a**gain he made David the target of his spear. This time David moved out of the pal**a**ce so the heartless king could not find him.

Jonathan helped his friend
  David hide
*Far from King Saul in **a** secret*
  place.
*It w**a**s hard for David to live*
  alone,
So the boys often met
  face-to-face. . . .

Even though Saul's hate
*would never **a**llow*
These two good friends to be
seen together.
*The boys **a**greed that, no*
matter what happened,
They would be friends forever
and ever.

As they parted, David promised Jon that he would always love Jon**a**th**a**n's family and care for them.

And he did!

Words that tickle your tongue
Find these words in the story and say them again: hurrah, *oohs* and *aahs*.

More phonics fun
Read this story again and find every **e** that sounds like the **e** in Israel and every **o** that sounds like the **o** in Goliath.

c, k, ck

c as in cat
k as in king
ck as in back

How Can a King Become Wise?

1 Kings 3

How can a king become wise? He can ask for a kind heart and for wisdom to know what is good and what is evil.

Solomon cared about his people. God promised to give Solomon anything he wanted. Solomon did not ask for a long life, or for riches, or for God to kill his enemies. Because of that, God made him rich and important and wise!

Just how wise could King Solomon be?
Read this story, and then you will see.

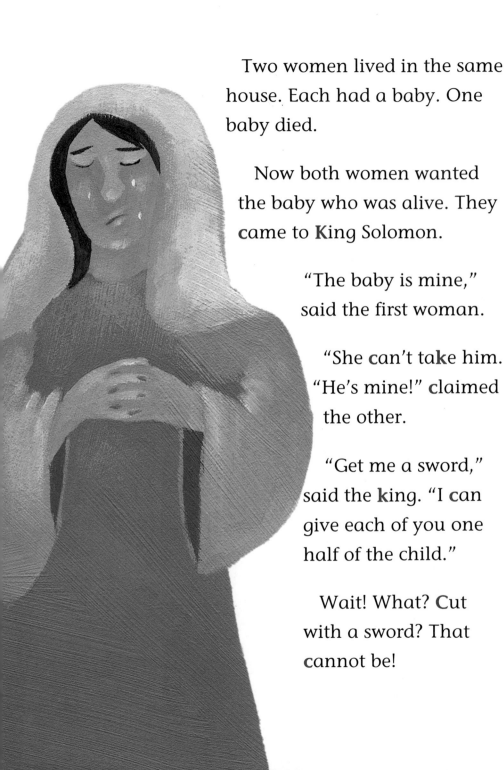

Two women lived in the same house. Each had a baby. One baby died.

Now both women wanted the baby who was alive. They came to King Solomon.

"The baby is mine," said the first woman.

"She can't take him. "He's mine!" claimed the other.

"Get me a sword," said the king. "I can give each of you one half of the child."

Wait! What? Cut with a sword? That cannot be!

*Is this **k**ing berser**k**? What is he thinking?*
*It's o**k**ay. . . . Don't **c**ry. Dry your tears and stop*
  *blin**k**ing.*
*It's not going to happen. The **k**ing*
  *is just ma**k**ing*
A way to find out which mother
  *is fa**k**ing.*
*So pi**ck** up your jaw. Tu**ck** your*
  *eyes ba**ck** in place.*
*This story's not gory. **K**eep a*
  smile on your face.

"Oh no! Do not hurt
the baby!" **c**ried the
first mother. "I **c**an't
bear it."

"I don't **c**are," said
the se**c**ond mother.
"It's just fine with me.
Do what you said.
Then NO ONE
will have a child."

Wise **King** Solomon gave the baby to the first woman. He knew she was the child's real mother.

How could he tell?
How did he know?
The REAL mom, of course,
Was the one who cried, "No!"

Words that tickle your tongue
Find these words in the story and say them again: blinking, faking.

Waters Dry Up and Weird Things Happen, but God Works Wonders

1 Kings 17

After King Solomon died, God's people began to have trouble. So they turned away from God to worship idols—gods that were not real. And then, guess what! Their troubles doubled!

God got angry with the people. And he sent Elijah to give them a warning. These were God's words:

"Because you are wicked
The rains will soon stop.
There won't be a drop
Of water to mop—
No water to drink
Or to wash feet and hands.
A famine will come
To all of your lands.
And Elijah's the only
One who can end it.
The rain will return when
He asks me to send it!"

Well, things were bad.
The people were mad.
They were filled with hate
And they could not wait
    To kill Elijah.

God sent him away
And told him to stay
Close to a brook
Where no one would look,
    And he would be safe.

He was in God's care.
His food came by air.
Each day of the week,
In a raven's beak,
    Came bread and meat.

Then the water in the brook dried up, and no crops would grow. A great famine came to the land. So God sent Elijah to a city.

Outside the city walls Elijah met a woman who was at work gathering sticks. He called to her:

"Please bring me some water
  And a piece of bread."
"I will give you the water,
  But I'm sorry," she said,
"That a wee bit of oil
  And a cup of grain
Is all I have left.
  Until there is rain
There won't be enough
  For my son and me.
If we share, we surely
  Will starve, you see."

"Go to your house," said Elijah. "Use the oil and grain you have to make some bread for me. Then you will see something wonderful happen."

The woman went away to bake the bread. She brought a loaf to Elijah. Then she went home and found plenty of oil and grain left to make more bread for herself and her son.

"See," said Elijah, "You won't need to worry.
Your grain will keep growing all by itself.
Bake what you need, for your oil won't run out,
And you will have plenty of food on your shelf."

Elijah was telling the truth! Day after day the woman would watch as her empty jars of oil and grain would fill themselves up again. It was a miracle!

But then something weird happened:

Suddenly the woman's son
Became so sick he died.
"He was well. Now he is dead!"
The boy's poor mother cried.

Sad at heart, Elijah laid
The boy upon his bed.
Then Elijah talked to God.
This is what he said:
"Wake this boy up from the dead,
And let the child revive.
Help this weeping woman. Help
Her son to come alive!"

God said yes, so then Elijah
Had good news to tell.
He found the mother, and he said,
"Look! Your son is well!"

The mother was so overjoyed that her eyes were wet with happy tears. She said to Elijah, "Now I know for sure that you are a man of God and that his words are true."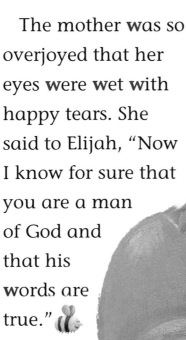

Words that tickle your tongue
Find these words in the story and say them again: miracle, weird.

Four Hundred Fifty Prophets Begging for Fire Are Not Enough!

1 Kings 18

For three long years there had been no rain in Israel. The king and the people were angry. They blamed God and Elijah for the famine, and they worshiped a false god named Baal.

Elijah told the king to call all the people and the four hundred fifty prophets of Baal to a contest. Elijah said to the people, "You cannot worship two gods. Let us have a fair contest to find out who is the true God—God or Baal.

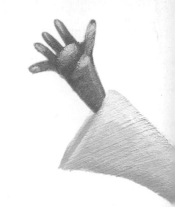

"Find two bulls and bring them here.
Each of us will lay just one
Upon an altar for our god.
Then get ready for some fun!

"After we have gathered wood,
We'll do something rather odd.
Instead of starting fires, each
Will pray for fire from his god.

"The god who hears and sends down fire
Will win the contest—that's the deal.
The god whose fire can burn the bull
Will give us proof that he is real!

"You go first," Elijah called to the prophets of Baal. So the four hundred fifty prophets put the meat from one bull on Baal's altar. They put a full load of wood under it. Then they began to pray.

"Oh, Baal, hear us!" they cried. They danced around the altar, leaping up and down.

174

They begged and bawled and shouted from
morning until noon, but their god refused to
answer. There was no fire. Elijah began
to laugh and laugh.

"Maybe your god is busy," he said.
"Or maybe he's far away.
Maybe he is half asleep
And cannot hear you say
How much you need his fire now!
To hear you may be tough—
Perhaps your prayers can't get
   to him
If they aren't loud enough!"

Elijah let out a great guffaw.
(That's a laugh and a half!)
So the prophets of Baal
yelled even louder.

They huffed and puffed as they danced faster and faster around the altar. But Baal seemed to be wearing earmuffs.

Then Elijah built an altar to God and put wood on it. He laid the meat from his bull on the wood. Elijah told the people to fill four barrels with water. He said,

"Pour all of the water on the dry wood.
And just to be very sure it is good
And wet, please do it again—and again
To make it all soggy and soaked." And then
He began to speak to the God he adored.
Elijah prayed by the altar, "Oh, Lord,
Please hear me so all these people will know
That you are the true God." Oh, what a show
God's fire made as it flashed from the skies.
The people could hardly believe their eyes.
It burned up the wood and the bull's meat and
*   bones.*
It licked up the water and even the stones!

When the people saw the fire, they fell with their faces to the ground and shouted, "The Lord is God! The Lord is God!"

Then Elijah went up on the mountain to pray for rain. Soon there were puffs of black cloud, and a great wind brought more proof of God's power. Rain began to fall, making a terrific storm. Soon the plants came back to life. The famine was over!

Words that tickle your tongue
Find these words in the story and say them again: guffaw, huffed, puffed, flashed.

More phonics fun
Read this story again to find every **ph** that sounds like the **ph** in al**ph**abet and every **gh** that sounds like the **gh** in laugh.

A **Wh**istle, a **Wh**irl, and a **Wh**inny—Elijah's Wild Chariot Ride

2 Kings 2

What a busy life Elijah had lived! But the time finally came **wh**en God was going to take Elijah away to heaven. So Elijah chose a new helper to take over his job. The helper's name sounded almost like Elijah's name. It was Elisha.

One day Elijah and Elisha were walking together. Some students asked Elisha, "Don't you know that God is coming to get Elijah today?"

181

Elisha did NOT want to hear these words.
He said to Elijah, "Hold on now! Steady!
Wherever you go, I want to be there.
Don't leave me. You know that I am not ready!"

Soon they came to the Jordan River. The waters were deep and wide, and there was no bridge on which to cross.

Elijah took off his coat and rolled it up. He whipped the water with it.

WHAM!
SLAM!
BAM!

Elisha wondered what Elijah was doing when, to his amazement, the water rolled back to make a path where the two could walk. So they crossed the river on dry land.

When they had
crossed, Elijah said to Elisha,
"What can I do for you
before I leave you?"

Elisha said, "The power that
God gave to you is super.
My wish is to have TWICE
    as much—
The kind that's super-
    duper!"

"Okay, my friend!"
    Elijah smiled.
"That should not be
    any trouble.
If you see God
    when he takes me,
Your power will
    be double!"

Then suddenly, Elisha got
the surprise of his life!

Out of nowhere, a
    fiery wind,
Whipping,
    whistling,
    whirling,
And a chariot of
    flaming fire,
Sweeping, swooping,
    swirling,
Appeared in the
    clouds as a
    horse's **whinny**
Was heard across
    the skies.
A **whirlwind**
    whisked Elijah
    away
In front of Elisha's
    eyes.

"My father!" Elisha cried out loud
As the chariot disappeared.
*"**Wh**ew!" he thought. "**Wh**at a wonder I've seen!*
How wild! How strange! How weird!"

Then he picked up Elijah's coat from the ground and walked back to the Jordan River. Just as Elijah had done, he hit the water with the coat.

***WH**AM!*
SLAM!
BAM!

The water parted, and Elisha crossed over to the other side.

When the students who were watching nearby saw **wh**at happened, they bowed down before Elisha and said, "The spirit of Elijah is now in Elisha." They were right. After that, God's power was with Elisha **wh**erever he went.

Words that tickle your tongue
Find these words in the story and say them again:
whinny, **wh**irlwind, **wh**isked, **Wh**ew!

A Jar of Oil, a Boy Made New, and Poison Veggies in a Pot of Stew!

2 Kings 3–4

Elisha was a good choice for a prophet to take Elijah's place! People could see that God's power was with him. And with God's power, he could do amazing things.

2 KINGS 3:15

A widow owed a man some money,
But she could not pay.
"Help!" she cried. "This man will take
My boys for slaves today."

To help the woman, Elisha asked,
"What do you have to sell?"
"Only one jar of oil!" she said.

He smiled. "Then all is well!
Get lots and lots of empty pots
And fill them from your jar.
*Your **oi**l will keep on filling up*
Those pots until there are
Enough to sell so that you can
Pay back all that you owe.
*Rej**oi**ce! Your bills can now be paid.*
*Your **boy**s won't have to go!"*   2 KINGS 4:1-7

Another time, Elisha heard
A woman's voice. She cried,
"The only boy God gave to me
Is gone now. He has died!"

So Elisha went to the bedroom. He put his
hands on the boy's hands, his eyes on the boy's
eyes, and his mouth on the boy's mouth. The
boy's body began to feel warm.

"ACHOO!" The boy made a noise that brought joy to Elisha's ears. The child sneezed seven times, then opened his eyes!

The mother rejoiced as she carried her son out. Elisha had used God's power to bring a boy back to life, just as Elijah had once done.

2 KINGS 4:8-37

Later Elisha went
    to a school.
They asked him to
    stay for lunch.
The cooks went to the
    garden to pick
Some vegetables by the bunch.

The veggies were put in a great big pot
And there they boiled and boiled.
But the students said the veggies tasted
Yucky! Rotten! Spoiled!

By some mistake
  some poison
  veggies
Got into the
  vegetable stew.
But Elisha said,
  "Don't be
  annoyed,
For God will take
  care of you."
He ordered the cooks
  to add to the stew
A tiny pinch of flour.
"Enjoy!" he said.
  "This stew is safe
Because of God's
  great power!"

Can't you just hear Elisha
and the students **noi**sily
slurping big spoonfuls of that
b**oi**led veggie stew? 2 KINGS 4:38-41

Words that tickle your tongue
Find these words in the story and say them again:
p**oi**son, re**joi**ce, vegetables, yucky.

The Healing
of a Strong Soldier

2 Kings 5

God's power was at work in his prophet,
Elisha.

In the streets of Israel, people were
    talking.
They were ooh-ing and ahh-ing,
    pointing and gawking.
To Elisha the prophet, many
    were flocking,
For the things
    God helped
    him to do were
    shocking.

But it was in another land called Syria that God had a young servant girl tell her master's wife about Elisha. The master's name was Naaman.

He had been suffering a long time with a terrible disease called leprosy. He had white, scaly sores all over his body. It looked like a fungus was growing on his skin. Naaman was a strong soldier, but he could do nothing about his leprosy.

So Naaman went to Syria's king.
The king gave him a letter
Asking Israel's king for help
In making Naaman better.
Then Naaman packed his chariot
With silver and with gold.
He went rushing off to Israel,
The place where he was told

Elisha could cure leprosy.
But at Elisha's door
The prophet sent a servant out
To say, "Off to the shore
Of River Jordan you must go
And seven times, dip in
The water. Then your leprosy
Will vanish from your skin!"

Naaman was getti**ng** angry. What kind of heali**ng** was this? He had been drivi**ng** for a lo**ng** time. Dippi**ng** in the dirty old Jordan River did not sound anythi**ng** like a cure. "I'm goi**ng** home!" he said, and he began turni**ng** his chariot around.

But the men who were with Naaman said to him, "If Elisha were telli**ng** you to do somethi**ng** hard, you would go alo**ng** with him and do it. So why not try this simple thi**ng**?"

"Well, okay," said Naaman.

"Since I am dying,
What's wrong with trying?"

Then he said, "I might as well head for the river." And he swung his chariot around.

Off to the river, he went tripping.
Down in the water, he went dipping.
Out of the water, he came dripping.
He looked at his skin and started
skipping!

Leaping onto his horse, he made a lickety-split trip back to Elisha's house. "Now I know that the God of Israel is the only God in the whole world," he said. He kept thanking Elisha and trying to give him gifts of gold and silver.

But Elisha knew the thanksgiving belonged to God. "No gifts for me," he said to Naaman. "Go in peace!"

Words that tickle your tongue
Find these words in the story and say them again: dipping, tripping, dripping, skipping, lickety-split.

Esther—The Girl Who Became Part of God's Perfect Plan

The book of Esther

After many years of war, some Jewish people had to live in other countries. One of these people was a beautiful girl named Esther.

Esther lived with her cousin Mordecai (MOR-duh-kye), who had taken care of her since her parents died. The leader of the country where Esther and Mordecai lived was powerful King Xerxes. (Say his name like this: ZERK-zees.)

King Xerxes thought he should have a better wife. He sent his servants to search for a another woman to be his new queen.

All over the kingdom,
Servants were seen
Looking for girls
Who could become queen.
Beautiful Esther
Was chosen to live
In the king's palace
Where servants would give
Her food and fine clothes,
Perfumes and creams—
All the wonderful stuff
Of a young girl's dreams.

Then one day Esther was called to see King Xerxes. The king loved her. So he set a royal crown on her head, and he made Esther his new queen.

Meantime, Mordecai
Was at the palace gate.
He overheard two guards
Who said, "How much we hate
The king. He is so bossy!
Let us make a plan
To kill him!" Mordecai
Got up, and then he ran
To tell the queen this
news.
She told the king! Oh, my.
In time the evil guards
Were sent outside to die.

King Xerxes was so busy, he forgot to
thank Mordecai for saving his life. Later,
the king chose a man named Haman
to be his honored helper. Xerxes
commanded that everyone had to bow
down to honor Haman.

Mordecai would not bow to him. Mordecai was Jewish and would only bow to God. So Haman thought of a dirty trick that would be certain to get rid of every Jewish person in the kingdom.

Haman told King Xerxes, "The Jewish people do not serve you well. They have the nerve to disobey your laws. I urge you to destroy them."

"Do as you wish," said the king. And he gave Haman his royal ring to seal the order that all Jews should be killed on a certain day.

When Mordecai heard of the plan,
He wrote this note and cried,
"Dear Esther, only you can help
Because you live inside
The palace. And I really hope
That you will tell the king
To stop this evil order that
Is sealed with his own ring."

But everyone knew about
   the rules.
So no one had to guess
That even the queen could not go in
To see the king unless
He called her to his room or raised
His scepter (SEP-ter) when she came.
If she displeased him, she would die.
Now that would be a shame!

   Esther asked Mordecai to gather all the Jews
to pray for her. Then she would go to King
Xerxes to beg for her life and the lives of her
people. "If I die, I die," she thought. "But I
must try!"

Perhaps God had put her in the palace just for this purpose. But Esther was worried because the king had not asked to see her for 30 days.

Esther was nervous. She put on her robes.
She entered King Xerxes' hall.
When he lifted his scepter to welcome her,
She suddenly understood all
The reasons God had chosen her
To be King Xerxes' queen—
So she could save her people and
God's power would be seen.

When Queen Esther asked Xerxes to save her life and the lives of all the Jews, the king let Queen Esther make a new rule that would save the Jews. First the king honored Mordecai for saving his life when his two guards had wanted to kill him. Then he sent evil Haman away to be hanged.

Esther was overjoyed to have been part of God's perfect plan!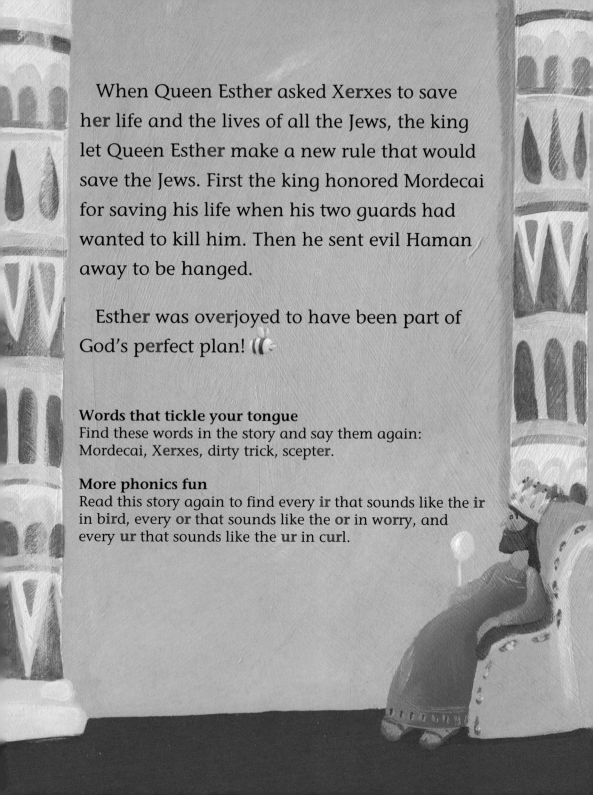

Think Joy! Shout Hallelujah!

Psalm One Hundred

God loves it when **h**is children sing to **h**im and talk with **h**im. Psalms are songs and prayers to God. Psalm One **H**undred is a psalm of worship and thanksgiving.

Hey everybody!
Think happy! Think joy!
Shout to the Lord—
Every girl, every boy.
Shout hallelujah!
Holler amen!
Do it together.
Now do it again!

211

Clap for **him**. Smile for **him**.
Just do your part.
Laugh for **him**. Sing to **him**
With all your **heart**!

Know this! **He** is God.
He made us, and we
Did NOT make **him**.
How amazing to see
That **he** knows
us and loves us.
We are **his** sheep.
He cares for us when we're
Awake or asleep.

Come to **his** house
And be at **h**ome there.
Praise **him** and thank **him**
For inviting you where
You will be loved forever.
O praise **him** and then
Sing **h**allelujah!
Hallelujah! Amen!

Words that tickle your tongue
Find these words in the story and
say them again: **h**allelujah,
psalm, **h**undred, **h**oller.

are, air, ar

are as in care
air as in hair
ar as in scary

A Library of Wise Sayings to Share

The book of Proverbs

The book of Proverbs is like a library of sayings that are wise and true. Listen carefully to these wise words of King Solomon.

If you carry them with you
Everywhere,
They will help you know
What is right and fair.

PROVERBS 1:3

215

Bew**are** of bad people who want you to go their way. Tear yourself away from them.

Don't be fooled.
*Their ways are sc**ary**!*
Don't listen to them.
*Be very w**ary**!* PROVERBS 1:10-19

When you act like a grouch, your day will be gloomy. When you are cheerful, your day will be like fresh **air** and sunshine.

Don't grump and groan
*And gripe and gl**are**.*
But find a happy
Smile to wear.
'Cuz if you want
A day that's merry,
A cheerful heart
*Is necess**ary**!* PROVERBS 15:15

Pay very close attention to what your parents tell you. Do not ever forget what they have taught you.

Wear their words
Everywhere—
Like a flower
In your hair.
Or on your finger
Like a ring,
So you won't
Forget a thing!

PROVERBS 1:8-9

217

A **pair** of lazy hands makes a person poor. But hard work can make a person a million**aire**.

If you are lazy,
If you're a slouch,
You won't have money
To put in your pouch!

But if you work hard
You'll have clothes to wear,
And you will have plenty
*Of good things to sh**are**.*   PROVERBS 10:4

You can tell about the char**acter** (**CARE**-ick-ter) of a child by the way he or she acts.

Even a child is known by his doings—
Whether he's kind and good at sharing
Or rude and sassy, pig-headed, pushy,
Mean and selfish—or just
   uncaring.   PROVERBS 20:11

   Children who are good and wise
make their parents proud.
Children who are foolish and
disobedient make their parents
sad.

Children who obey will have
A merry Mom and Dad.
Children who are stubborn will have
Parents who are sad!　　　PROVERBS 10:1

Trust God with all your heart. Do not try to **carry** on by yourself. Ask what God wants you to do, and he will show you.

Listen closely to God's voice.
His way should be your only choice.
*His ideas you should sh**are**.*
He'll go with you everywhere!　　　PROVERBS 3:5-6

Words that tickle your tongue
Find these words in the story and say them again:
lib**rary**, Proverbs, necess**ary**, pig-headed.

More phonics fun
Read the proverbs again to find every **ear** that sounds like the **ear** in b**ear**, every **eir** that sounds like the **eir** in th**eir**, and every **er** that sounds like the **er** in v**er**y.

Three Brave Boys Will Not Bow Down to the Sound of Music

Daniel 1–3

Nebuchadnezzar (neb-uh-cud-NEZ-ur) was the king of Babylon. He liked Daniel because Daniel could explain what God said about the king's strange dreams. The king made Daniel the ruler over all of Babylon.

Daniel and his friends Shadrach, Meshach, and Abednego had been brought out of Israel.

They came to Babylon to be slaves in the king's house. Some of the king's men pouted and frowned when the king asked Daniel's friends to be important helpers.

One day Nebuchadnezzar gave orders to build a huge gold statue (STAT-choo). He commanded his helpers to bow down to worship the statue whenever they heard the sound of loud music.

When the music was loud,
Everyone bowed.
As the music played,
Everyone prayed—

Well, ALMOST everyone . . .

There were three in the crowd
Who NEVER bowed.
They were Daniel's friends,
And they would bend
Only to God.
How right! How odd!

At least it seemed odd, for in the middle of
that bowed-down crowd, the boys stuck out like
three tall towers. So the king's jealous men
tattled on Shadrach, Meshach, and Abednego.

The king flew into a wild rage.

He scowled.
He howled.
He grumped.
He growled.

"If you do not **bow do**wn to worship as I command you, I will have you tossed into a fiery furnace!" he sh**ou**ted.

The three friends were not afraid. They knew that God was with them. And when the music played, they stood tall and pr**ou**d. The king roared,

*"So you won't **bow down**
When you hear my band?
You'll be tossed to the fire!
That is my command."*

*The friends spoke politely,
"We can't **bow** to your cr**ow**n.
But **ou**r God will save us.
He won't let us d**ow**n."*

N**ow** the king sc**ow**led and gr**ow**led even more. "Heat the furnace seven times hotter!" he sh**ou**ted. And then he told his men to throw the friends into the roaring flames.

*The boys didn't sc**ow**l.
They didn't sh**ou**t.
They didn't h**ow**l.
     They didn't p**ou**t.*

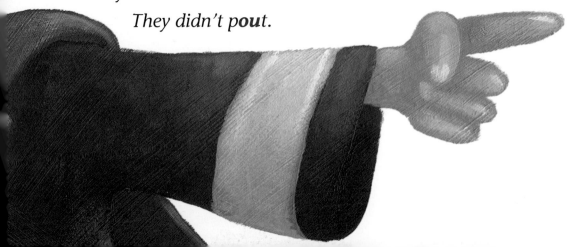

And best of all,
They didn't doubt.
They didn't even
Try to get out!

The king could not believe his eyes. As he watched the three boys standing in the fire with flames all around them, he saw that they were not harmed. Also, he believed he saw a fourth person standing with them. He had to count to be sure. Could this person be the Son of God?

Then the king ordered,
"Come out of there!"
Quickly he saw
That not a hair
Was burned by the flames,
And not one cloak
Had even been touched
By the fire or smoke!

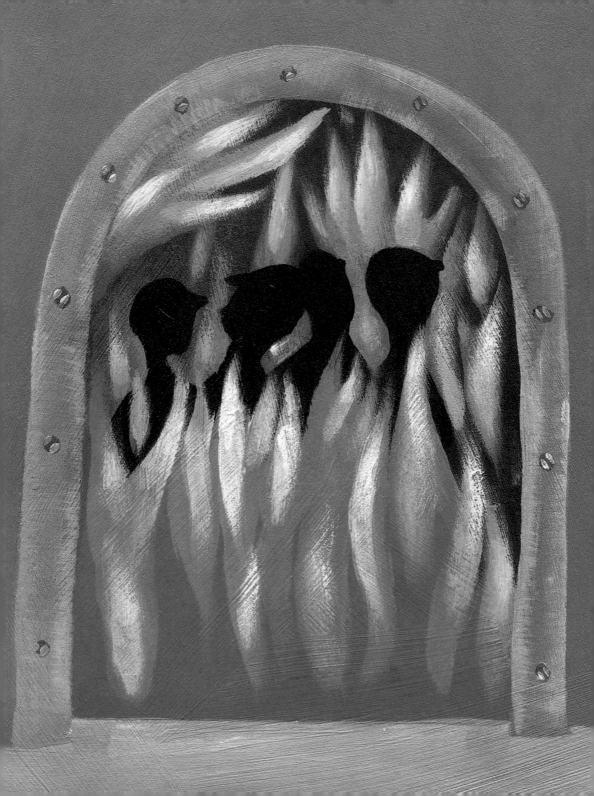

The king was dumbfounded! (That means he was too surprised to speak.) "Wow!" he thought. "The God of these Hebrew boys must be SOME AWESOME GOD!"

Then the king announced loudly, "I will never let anyone say anything against the God of Shadrach, Meshach, and Abednego." He gave the three friends jobs of great power in his kingdom.

How about that? God wins again!

Words that tickle your tongue
Find these words in the story and say them again:
Nebuchadnezzar, Shadrach, Meshach, and Abednego,
    dumbfounded.

No Small, Silly Law . . .
No Big Lion's Jaw . . .
Can Keep Daniel
from Talking to God

Daniel 6

Daniel had a new boss. His name was King Darius, and Daniel was his favorite helper. This made the king's other helpers cross and jealous. They all began to talk about how they could get Daniel in trouble with the king.

*"Oh king," they said. "You are so
  great.
Now here's what you should
  do.
Make this law: No one can
  pray
To anyone but you.*

231

Should someone in your kingdom not
Obey, then call your men,
And order them to toss him down
Into the lions' den."

The king liked the idea. If he made the new law, he would get all the attention. He wrote the law on paper so that no one could change it. Not even the boss—himself!

As soon as the law was signed, Daniel's enemies walked across the palace grounds to Daniel's house. They all stood by the wall outside his window. They knew that Daniel prayed there three times a day—at dawn, at noon, and at night.

This day was no different. Daniel began talking to his God by the small window in the wall of his room.

When the men heard Daniel praying, they
All rushed to tell the king.

The king was ticked. He had been tricked,
But he couldn't do a thing.
"Why did I listen to silly talk?
My brain is full of beans!
These hungry lions' jaws will tear
Poor Dan to smithereens!"

(That means into millions of tiny pieces!)

But the law was the law, and even the king could not change it. The king bawled while the men walked Daniel to the lions' den and tossed him in. Then they rolled a big stone across the door of the den.

They were proud that they had double-crossed both Daniel and the king.

All night long the king tossed and turned. He could not sleep—not even a small wink. At dawn he rushed to the door of the lions' den.

When he looked into the den,
This is what he saw—
Daniel walking tall and strong,
Untouched by tooth or claw.

"Daniel! Daniel!" called the king.
"I'm sorry about that law!"
"Don't worry!" answered Daniel.
"God shut the lions' jaws."

The king was so overjoyed, his heart must have bounced like a ball. He called some men to lift Daniel out of the den of lions. Then he had the bad men thrown into the den.

Once again, all of the kingdom heard about God's awesome power!

Words that tickle your tongue
Find this word in the story and say it
again: smithereens.

More phonics fun
Read this story again and find every **o** that
sounds like the **o** in cr**o**ss.

Jonah Tries to Hide from God—Ha! He Doesn't Get Very Far . . .

The book of Jonah

When God says, "GO!" it's smart to say,
"Yes Sir! As you wish!"
Or, like old Jonah, you may be
Swallowed by a fish!

God told Jonah to go to the wicked city of Nineveh to preach. But Jonah ran away from God and went to the city of Joppa, where he got on a ship to sail to a town called Tarshish.

The ship had hardly left the harbor when God sent a wild wind to stir up the sea.

Jonah went down below the deck to take a nap. While he snoozed, the boat was tossed like a piece of bark on the waves. Everything started to fall apart. The sailors were alarmed.

"Wake up, Jonah!" the sailors cried.
"A frightful storm is brewing.
Our ship is going to break apart.
Just WHAT is your God doing?"

"I'm to blame," said Jonah.
"God's orders I ignored.
I'm the one who caused this harm,
So toss me overboard!"

"The sharks may eat you," cried the crew.
But Jonah hollered, "Hurry!
Get rid of me. The storm will stop.
Then you won't have to worry!"

The sailors squabbled among themselves about throwing Jonah into the wild sea. They thought God might be angry with them for tossing Jonah to the sharks.

It was hard for them, but Jonah said, "If you are smart, you will do what I ask." So the sailors took Jonah by the arms and legs and swung him up and over the side of the ship—far out into the deep, dark waters.

Tah-dah! Oh yes!
   God did his part.
He sent a giant fish
To swallow Jonah, who then prayed,
"Lord, I know what you wish.

You heard my cries. You saved
my life.
I WILL obey your ways."
And Jonah stayed
unharmed inside
The fish three nights
and days!

And then that large sea animal
Began to swim toward land.
Hurrah! He spit old Jonah out—
Kerplunk—upon the sand.
Oh, what a ride! How Jonah shivered.
Then he heard God's voice:
"Now you go on to Nineveh
To preach! You are my choice."

So off Jonah marched to take God's message
to the people of Nineveh. He felt ashamed for
running away from God's commands.

God knows best.
He does his part.
To let him be
In charge is smart!

Note: The official way to say the name *Jonah* is "JO-nuh." However, because it is spelled with an "**ah**," most people say "JO-n**ah**." So in the story we have put in color the **a** in Jon**a**h.

Words that tickle your tongue
Find these words in the story and say them again:
Nineveh, Joppa, T**a**rshish, squ**a**bbled, tah-d**a**h, kerplunk.

NEW TESTAMENT 🐝

An Angel Arrives with Marvelous News

Matthew 1:18-25; Luke 1:26-38

"A baby is coming! A baby is coming! And you are going to be the baby's mother."

The young virgin Mary could see a stranger standing in front of her. She could hear a voice speaking to her. But she could not believe her eyes or ears.

Who was this visitor?
How DID he arrive?
Where did he come from?
Was he alive?

Perhaps she was dreaming.
Had she just gone to sleep?
Or would she now have
A big secret to keep?
For what she had heard,
She dared not believe.
She wanted to hide
Her face in her sleeve.

But the visitor spoke again. "Do not be afraid, Mary. I am Gabriel, and God sent me to give you this message. You are a most favored person of God. He chose you to have his baby Son. You will name the baby Jesus. He will be a great king, and his kingdom will last forever."

"How can this happen?
How can it be?
I'm just a young girl—
A virgin, you see—
And he is my God.
How can this come true?"

"God's power," said Gabriel,
"Will come over you."

Then Mary spoke softly.
She nodded her head.
"Yes, I am God's servant.
Let it be as you said."

When the angel was
gone, Mary wondered
how she would ever find
the nerve to tell Joseph.
She and Joseph were to
be married very soon.
She knew Joseph loved
her, but she was sure
no person alive would
ever believe THIS
story!

Happily, Mary was **very** wrong. Gabriel soon arrived at the place where Joseph lived. Joseph was asleep, but the angel did not need to have anyone let him in the door.

He came to Joseph in a dream
And said, "Don't be afraid.
The child that Mary soon will have
Is one that God has made.
And when her baby son is born,
You'll give this little boy
The name of Jesus. He will save
The world and bring great joy."

What a dream!
Joseph was dizzy.
Then he woke up,
And he got busy.

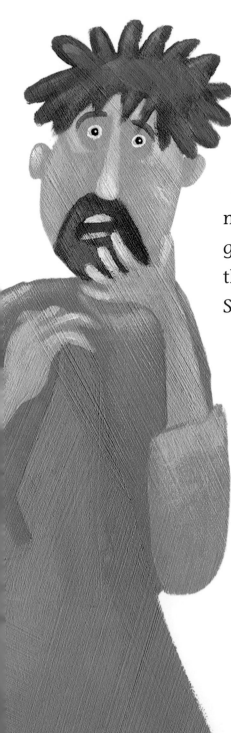

He took Mary
To be his wife,
And they were the parents
During Jesus' young life.

But they never, ever—not in a million years—could have guessed what marvelous things this child would do as the Savior of the world.

Words that tickle your tongue
Find these words in the story and say them again: marvelous, virgin, visitor, nerve, dizzy, Savior.

A Savior **Sh**ares a Borrowed **Sh**ed

Luke 2:1-20

It was a hurry, scurry, busy, dizzy night in the little town of Bethlehem.

*Hundreds of **sh**oppers filled the street.*
*Sellers were **sh**outing, "Stop here to eat!*
*We have lentil soup and fi**sh** to fry*
And a dozen kinds of cakes to buy!"
There were soldiers on horses and donkeys with
  carts,
And camels with all of their slow-moving parts.
They could run you down if you didn't
    watch out.
*Now, what was all of this ru**sh**ing about?*

255

A new law said that every Jewish person must go to the city where his family first started. He had to be counted and write his name in a big book. Mary and Joseph were two of the many, many visitors coming to Bethlehem on this wild night. And they were in a hurry. Mary's baby was about to be born, but they had no place to stay.

KNOCK KNOCK! Joseph banged on the old hotel
* door.*
"Go away!" said the owner. "There are no more
Empty rooms at this place. There is only a shed
Where I keep the cows—and there is no bed!"

Then Mary cried out, "The baby is coming!"
Well, that old innkeeper, he got humming.

"Young lady," he said, "grab hold of my shoulder.
And you, sir, get over here! Help me hold her!"
So off they shuffled to find the shed
Where Mary could lay her tired head.

At that very moment, outside of Bethlehem in a big, dark field, a bunch of sleepy **shepherds** were taking care of their **sheep**.

SHAZAAM! A huge, bright light suddenly began to **shine** in the sky above them.

SWOOSH! The **sh**epherds heard a ru**sh**ing sound. Their **sheep** huddled together.

The **sh**epherds pulled their **sh**awls tightly around their **sh**oulders and fell to their knees, **sh**ivering and **sh**uddering and **sh**aking with

fright. They covered their eyes to **sh**ield them from the bright light. Then, in the **sh**ining light, they saw an angel.

"Be not afraid," the angel said.
"Do not **sh**iver and **sh**udder with dread.
There is no reason to **sh**ake with fright,
For unto you is born this night
A Savior. He's **sh**aring a borrowed **sh**ed
With cows and **sh**eep. And his little head
Lies in a manger. He's wrapped in a **sh**eet."
Then before the **sh**epherds could stand on their feet . . .

WHOOSH! A whole sky full of angels appeared.
"Glory to God in the highest!" they cheered.
And they sang the most beautiful song ever heard.
Then after the angels had sung their last word,
The shepherds all dashed from their field through
  the street,
For THIS was a baby they wanted to meet!

Just as the angel had told them, they found Mary and Joseph and the baby safe in the borrowed shed. The baby Jesus was lying on the hay in a manger. When they saw the baby, the shepherds fell on their knees to worship him.

Shhh! The baby is sleeping. . . .

Words that tickle your tongue
Find these words in the story and say them again: innkeeper, shuffled, shepherd, huddled, shivering, shuddering, shield.

God Saves His Young Son from a Yucky King!

Matthew 2

Yikes! The most important person in the world had just been born, and already there was trouble! Jesus was still a young child when yucky King Herod became jealous of him.

Herod heard that some men from far away who studied the stars were asking, "Where is the baby who will become king of the Jews? We have seen his bright yellow star in the sky and have come to worship him."

Herod felt like yelping and yanking the hats off the heads of these visitors. He did not want to hear about a new king. Why, he might lose his job!

But this King Herod was no fool.
So he just smiled and kept his cool.
The words he spoke were calm and kind:
"Come, see me, gentlemen, when you find
This little child—this king so new.
For I must come and worship too!"

Oh, **yuck!** That's not what the king wanted to do at all.

Liar, liar—your pants are on fire!
Your nose is as long as a telephone wire!

(Except, of course, there weren't any telephone wires in those years!)

When the visitors left Herod's house, the bright yellow star appeared to them again, and they followed it to find Jesus. They bowed down to worship the young child. And they gave him gifts of gold and spices. Then God warned them not to return to Herod but to go home a different way.

The moment Herod heard that those stargazers were not coming back, he gave his soldiers orders to kill every young Jewish boy who was under two years old.

He was NOT going to lose his job—OH, NO!
So this little king would have to go.

While Herod was yapping and yakking about losing his job, yelling, "NO! NO! NO!" God sent an angel to tell Joseph not to worry. God was going to save the boy Jesus. YES! YES! YES!

God helped Mary and Joseph and their young child sneak away to the land of Egypt, where they stayed until yucky old King Herod died.

Words that tickle your tongue
Find these words in the story and say them again: liar, telephone wire, stargazers, yakking.

The Boy from Nazareth Is Thought to Be Lost

Luke 2:41-52

Every year Mary and Joseph traveled for several days from their town of Nazareth to the city of Jerusalem to celebrate the Passover. Thousands of people came to Jerusalem for this time of feasting and thanksgiving. Families and friends walked together or rode side by side on donkeys and horses.

The year when Jesus was twelve years old, Mary and Joseph thought they should all go to Passover together. But on the pathway home, something unthinkable happened:

The road back to Nazareth was very long.
At the end of the day, something seemed to be
   wrong.
The lines of travelers were crowded and thick,
And suddenly, Joseph felt terribly sick.

He hadn't seen Jesus since early that morning.
He **th**ought he had better give Mary some warning
That Jesus was missing. They bo**th** looked around,
But in **th**ousands of travelers, he couldn't be found.

So back to the city they went
in a hurry,
But another whole day had
passed—what a worry!
How sad to have lost their
twelve-year-old son.
They hoped he was just with
his friends, having fun.
Or perhaps he was **th**irsty
and stopped for a drink,
But now it was dark. Oh,
what could they **th**ink?

They searched **th**rough
Jerusalem all the **th**ird day.
They passed by the temple,
and suddenly they
Could see Jesus talking with
teachers in there.
His mother cried out, "We
have searched everywhere!"

She hugged him so hard,
 they were both out of
 breath.
"Don't you know you have
 nearly scared us to
 death?"

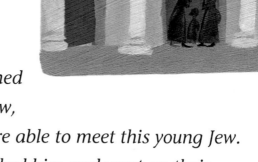

The teachers, astonished
 at what the boy knew,
Were thrilled they were able to meet this young Jew.
Most likely, they thanked him and went on their
 way.
And perhaps as they left him, they heard Jesus say,
"I'm sorry I caused you such worry and fear,
But Mom, did you not know that I would be here?"

At that moment, Mary did not understand
what Jesus meant. But later she remembered his
words, and then she knew. Of course Jesus
would want to be at the temple. It was his
heavenly Father's house on earth!

Jesus grew both wise and tall.
He was loved by God and all
Who knew him. And they
  watched him grow
Kind and gentle—
  head to toe.

Words that tickle your tongue
Find these words in the story and
say them again: Nazareth, Passover,
thousands, thanksgiving, unthinkable,
astonished.

Big John—the Man Who Wore Camel Hair and Leather

Matthew 3

Big John **the** Baptist lived outdoors in **the** desert. His clo**th**ing, made of camel hair, was held toge**th**er by a lea**th**er belt. He ate locusts, and honey made by **the** wild desert bees.

People came from all over **the** country to hear John talk about Jesus. He told **them** how to get ready for **the** Savior by turning away from **th**eir sins:

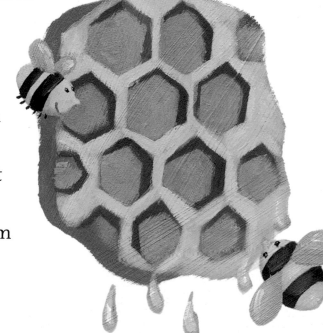

273

Along the Jordan riverside,
He told the crowds, "You cannot hide
Your sins. You must repent and pray
To be forgiven." That's the way
To know that you will go someday
To live with God in heaven—hooray!

"Confess your sins, then be baptized.
And don't be fooled—don't be surprised.
God will not save you just because
Of who your great-great-grandpa was!"
John also told each one to say
To God, "Oh, yes! I will obey."

Then John baptized many of the people in the Jordan River, and they traded their old, sinful lives for the new life that Jesus was ready to give them.

One day Jesus came to the Jordan River. He wanted John to baptize him, too.

John said, "That's backwards! You should be
The person who will baptize me!"

"You don't know all **that**'s
    on God's mind,"
Said Jesus. "Will you be
    so kind
As just to do what God has
    said?"
And so John did. **Then** overhead
The blue sky opened. It did seem
That from **the** heavens, like a dream,
A pure white dove wi**th** wings all spread
Came down to rest on Jesus' head.

*And **then** a voice spoke from above:*

*"**This is my Son, the one I love.**"*

Words that tickle your tongue
Find these words in the story and say them again: leather,
together, baptized, backwards.

Just a Touch from the Master

Matthew 8–9

News about Jesus spread quickly from town to town. Everybody was telling stories about how Jesus could make sick people well with just a touch.

"Hooray!" cried a man
As he danced in the street.
"I'm clean! No more sores
On my hands and my feet!
I just saw Jesus.
I cried, 'You're the man!
If you want to heal me,
I know that you can!'

"Then he touched me and said,
'I will heal you! Be clean.'
Now, is this not the prettiest
Skin you have seen?"

And this healed man went leaping—
He jumped up and down,
Shouting, "Jesus has made me
The cleanest in town!"

Whooping and hollering at the top of his lungs, the man pointed to his skin. He wanted to be sure everyone would see that Jesus had taken all his sores away. MATTHEW 8:1-4; MARK 1:40-45

Another time, as Jesus was talking with some friends of John the Baptist, a man came running toward him.

"Oh, Jesus," he said,
"My daughter has died,

But if you will touch her,
She'll live!" the man cried.

So right away, Jesus
Started out walking.
He came to the house
Where people were talking
And wondering just what
This Jesus could do.
He said, "Now, get out—
Every one of you!"
Then he took the girl's
    hand,
And she rose to her
    feet.
Oh, what a story
To tell in the street!

MATTHEW 9:14, 18, 23-26

On that same day, as Jesus was walking along with the large crowd, he felt someone touch his robe.

For twelve years a woman
Had been very sick.
Then she heard that Jesus
Was coming. "Be quick,"
She said to herself.
"I know I'll be well
If I just touch his robe.
He can't even tell
That I am behind him.
He'll never know."
But she was surprised
At what happened. Oh, no—
She did not fool Jesus—
Her secret he knew.
He turned and he said,
"Your faith has healed you!"

MATTHEW 9:19-22

Later, as Jesus was walking home, he was followed by two blind men. They called out to him:

"Master! Have mercy!
Oh, please make us see."
And Jesus said, "Since
You believe, let it be!"
So he touched them, putting
His hands on their eyes.
Then he said, "You are well,
And if you are wise,
You won't tell a soul
What I did on this day."
But the men went off shouting,
"Jesus DID it! HOORAY!"

The people Jesus healed just had to tell someone. They could NOT keep from talking about the miraculous things he did for them—with just a touch! 🐝 MATTHEW 9:27-31

Words that tickle your tongue
Find these words in the story and say them again: whooping, faith, miraculous.

285

_r

br as in bread, cr as in cry,
dr as in dry, fr as in fry, gr as in
grape, pr as in prize, tr as in tree

Four Friends Drop a Sick Man through a Hole in a Roof! Crazy!

Mark 2:1-12

One day Jesus was **pr**eaching in a house that was **cr**owded with so many people that they could hardly move or **br**eathe. Four men came to the door. They were **br**inging to Jesus a sick **fr**iend who could not move his arms and legs. But they had a **pr**oblem—a **gr**eat BIG **pr**oblem!

The **cr**owd in the house was **cr**unched together so tightly that the men could not get their **fr**iend through the **fr**ont door. They had to think of another way to get into the house. So they made a plan—**pr**obably something like this:

"We've got **trouble**!
On the double,
Grab the mat.
And keep it flat.
Don't let it **dr**op.
Then up to the top
Of the house we go.
To the roof!—
     HEAVE HO!"

   Very
carefully, they
dragged the
friend on his
mat up the long
stairway to the
roof. Then they did
something **tr**uly **cr**azy.

Quickly they moved
Some pieces of roof.
The **crowd** inside
Looked up—and
  POOF!
All of a sudden,
There was a door
Where there had
  been
A roof before!
Then slowly the mat
With the man was
  dropped
To the **gr**ound. In
  front
Of Jesus, it stopped.

Jesus was not surprised at all. He looked at the sick man and said, "Son, your sins are forgiven."

Some angry Jewish leaders in the **cr**owd **gr**umped and **gr**oaned. They thought Jesus had no right to forgive sins. Only God could do that! But Jesus knew what they were thinking, and he was **pr**epared to **pr**ove them wrong.

*"Don't **trouble** your **brains**,"*
Jesus said. "Do you
Not know what my Father
Has sent me to do?
Now see for yourselves
That I have God's power.
*While you are **grumping***
And looking sour,
My God-given power
*I will **prove**."*
Then he said to the sick man,
"Get up and move.

Take your mat
And walk away."
*Those **grumpy** jaws **dr**opped—*
They had nothing to say!

The **gr**eat **cr**owd watched
the man walk away. They knew
they had seen a miracle,
and they went **cr**azy—
praising God and
saying, "This Jesus
truly is the Son
of God!"

**Words that tickle your
tongue**
Find these words in the
story and say them again:
crazy, **cr**unched,
grumped, **gr**oaned.

Jesus Escapes on a Lake, and Fishermen Make a Change to Follow Jesus

Luke 5–6

"Who is this Jesus?"
"Have you heard? Do you know?"
"He amazes us all
Wherever we go!"

No one in Galilee had ever seen anything like Jesus' power! They all kept talking about him.

"Wherever he goes, he heals the lame,
Gives attention to any who call out his name.
Each time he speaks, people listen with care.
The crowd is so still, they don't move a hair."

It was true. Many people loved Jesus.

293

Sometimes hundreds came from a faraway place.
They walked for miles just to see his face.
Many came early—and stayed until late,
They didn't even care if they slept or ate.

It was hard for Jesus to find time alone.
Wherever he went, his name was known.
The people would race to get to his side.
Jesus had no place where he could hide.

More and more people were coming to see Jesus. It seemed there was no hillside large enough to hold them.

One day Jesus was standing by a lake. He was tired, and it was hard to speak to so many people at once. Then he noticed two boats tied up on the beach. The crowds were so eager to be near Jesus they were pushing—pushing him toward the lake. So he got into the boat that Peter owned.

He thought, "What a perfect
escape! This will float!"

"Hey, Peter!" he called.
"May I use your boat?
The people are pushing me.
They want to hear
What I have to say,
And they've crowded too near."

"Just untie the rope!"
Hollered Peter. "Let's go!"
Then he jumped in with Jesus
And started to row.
Now Jesus could speak
From the boat to the beach.
So the people sat down
To hear Jesus teach.

When he finished teaching,
Jesus said to Peter, "Let's ride
out a little farther into the
lake. Let your net slide down
into the deep water to catch
some fish."

"Oh, Master,"
said Peter,
with great
irritation,
"The fish must
have gone on
their summer
vacation!

We worked all night long and did not see ONE fish,
But we'll slide our nets over the side if you wish!"

Right away, the whole net was filled with
huge piles of fish. When Peter saw all those fine
fish, he fell to his knees in front of Jesus. He
knew that Jesus could do things that no other
man could do.

Then Jesus spoke to Peter; his brother, Andrew; and his friends James and John. "Follow me, and I will show you how to catch something better than fish—men, women, and children who want to hear about God."

The men pulled their boats up on the beach and left them there. They walked away with Jesus, and they became his very first disciples.   LUKE 5:1-11

Some time later, Jesus went up on a mountain and stayed there all night, praying. In the morning he called his disciples to come. From the whole bunch of them, he chose twelve special ones:

He first called Peter,
Then Andrew, his brother,
Then James, John, and Philip,
And then came another
With a very long name—
Bartholomew.
All six of them said,
"Yes, we'll follow you!"
Then he said, "Come, Matthew
And Thomas and James
And Simon"—then two more
Who had the same names—
Judas and Judas
Iscariot—they
Were the last of the twelve
Jesus chose on that day.

He called these twelve friends
His apostles, and then
He taught them all how
To be fishers of men.
They traveled with Jesus
Wherever he went.
And they learned what following
Jesus Christ meant.

LUKE 6:12-19

Words that tickle your tongue
Find these words in the story and say them again: escape, irritation, vacation, disciples, Bartholomew, Judas Iscariot, apostles.

many silent letters

e as in place, gh as in right,
h as in honor, k and w
as in know, l as in talk,
t as in listen, w as in wrong

Jesus Taught His Disciples How to Talk to God

Matthew 6:9-13; Luke 11:1-4
(The Lord's Prayer)

To our Daddy, who lives in a perfect place:

From earth we're not able to see your face.

But we know that you love us. We feel your care.

From heaven, you listen to every prayer.

Honor and glory to you we bring,

Oh, Mighty Maker of everything.

You must be sad about bad things
we do,

But when you come back, ALL
things will be new.

So we wait for this evil to pass
away,

And for you to return—such
a happy day!

301

We have messed up your earth. Now it is not good.
And we never obey your commands as we should.
We ignore your advice. We worry and fight.
How we wish it might be as you planned it—just
    right!

All that we have has come
        from you—
The sun and rain, our
        breakfast, too.
You give the clothing that we
    wear.
Today this is our quiet
        prayer:
        Give what we need—
            that is enough.
        (But thank you for the
            extra stuff!)

    Sometimes when I kneel
        to pray,
    A sigh comes with the
            words I say

Because I know the wrong I've done,
And bad things over good have won.
But you forgive and close your eyes
To my mistakes. Oh, God so wise,
To those who wrong me, I would be
As kind as you have been to me.

Down here on earth, things get
  confusing.
And we are not so good at choosing.
It's hard to tell the wrong from
  right.
But you have said that you
  are Light,
So please, Lord, shine your
  beam this way.
Show us our faults. And help
  us stay
Connected to our heavenly
  Dad—
Away from stuff we know
  is bad.

We may have done our best to be good,
But you are the only person who could
Be perfect. We honor you, give you praise.
Your power and glory, we worship always.

Bravo to our hero! Your name we will bless
Forever and ever and ever. Oh, yes!
Yes! Yes! Yes!

Words that tickle your tongue
Find these words in the story and say them again: confusing,
connected, bravo.

S_

sc as in scare, sk as in skin, sl as in
sleep, sm as in smile, sn as in snow,
sp as in spin, spl as in splash, st as in stop,
str as in street, sw as in sweet

Who Can Stop a Scary Storm with Just a Shout?

Matthew 8:23-27; Mark 4:35-41; Luke 8:22-25

One day when the **sky** was blue and the wind was **strong**, Jesus called to his friends, "Who wants to go for a ride in a boat?"

"Where will we go?" they asked.

"Let's sail across the lake," he said.

*A **spin** to take them*
Across the lake
Was a ride the disciples
All loved to take.

307

Sweeping and swooping
In wind so swift
Was fun. It would give
Their spirits a lift.

Jesus **sm**iled. His friends **sc**urried into the **sm**all boat. As soon as they were on their way, Jesus lay down to **sl**eep. Then the wind got **str**onger, and it began to **st**ir the water into a **st**ormy **st**ew.

The sky became
As black as night.

And all the men
Were sick with fright.
So they began
To hang on tight.

The wind blew the water into big waves.

Slam! Bam!
Smash! Crash! **Spl**ash!

The waves **sw**ished and **sw**irled the little boat about as if it were only a **str**ing or a **str**aw on the water.

Whack! **Sm**ack!

The wind bumped and banged on the boat's bow. The disciples were scared that the wind would sweep them overboard. They were afraid that the waves would sneak up on them and swallow them up.

"Jesus, wake up!"
They shouted. "Be quick!
The storm is scary,
And we are sick!"

They were trying to steer,
But it wasn't easy.
Their stomachs were feeling
Strange and queasy.
At one giant splash,
They began to think
This boat full of water
Would surely sink.

Well, Jesus DID wake up. He stood up in the boat. "Stop!" he yelled at the swirling wind. "Be still!" he shouted to the waves.

At once, everything was quiet!

"Wow!" said the men. "Did you see that?" They stared in amazement. "Who is this man, anyway? Even the wind and the waves stop to listen when he speaks!"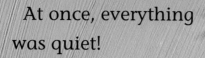

Note: The **sh** sound was featured before in the Luke 2 Christmas story. You'll see that those two letters are not in color in the above story because the two letters do not blend. They create one new sound.

Words that tickle your tongue
Find these words in the story and say them again: swooping, swished, swirled, swallow, stomachs, queasy.

tw,thr,qu

tw as in twelve,
thr as in three,
qu as in quake

Quite a Surprise
Seen through
Thousands of Eyes

Matthew 14:13-21; Mark 6:32-44; Luke 9:10-17; John 6:1-13

Jesus was the most popular man in Galilee, where he lived. Great **thr**ongs of people—big crowds—followed him and his **tw**elve disciples everywhere.

The **thr**ongs **qu**ivered with excitement as they watched him heal the sick, and they were **thr**illed to hear him teach.

One day Jesus and his friends were **qu**ite tired and tried to escape to a **qu**iet place. But the **thr**ongs of people **qu**ickly found them, and once again it was like a **thr**ee-ring circus. There were people to the right, people to the left, people EVERYWHERE!

So Jesus was busy, healing and teaching.
And all day long he was touching and reaching
To make the bodies of sick people well.
Then **qu**ietly, he began to tell
Them stories about his Father above,
And the peace they could find **thr**ough his Father's
   love.

Of course, such a day was not very easy,
At supper time everyone's stomach was **qu**easy.
The people were hungry, and nowhere near
Was there any market—not way out here!
No Wendy's, no Subway, no Burger King,
No McDonald's with toys. There was no such thing.

The worried disciples said, "What shall we do?"
And then Jesus answered (his teaching was
   through),
"**Qu**it **tw**iddling your thumbs. Be **qu**ick on your feet.
Please hurry! Go find us all something to eat!"

Through the crowd came a boy with five loaves and
two fish—
Just the stuff Jesus needed to make a fine dish.
And that dish would feed more than five thousand
men.
He held it up high to thank God, and then
He broke up the food into baskets to pass
To all of the people who sat on the grass.

They ate and they ate until everyone's tummy
Was full as could be. The food was just yummy!
*And when they were **through**, there were **twelve***
baskets more
Of leftover food they could take to the poor!

Imagine! Feeding a huge crowd with only five loaves of bread and two little fish. There was no **qu**estion that this man who could **thrill throngs** of people with such a miracle was truly God's Son.

Words that tickle your tongue
Find these words in the story and say them again: Galilee, throngs, thrilled, three-ring circus, twiddling, loaves.

_f, _k, _p

lf as in self, nk as in thank,
sk as in ask, lp as in help,
mp as in jump, sp as in gasp

Ask Yourself: "Am I a Good Neighbor?"

Luke 10:25-37

The Jews did not get along with their Samaritan neighbors. But this was not how Jesus taught his followers to think and act toward one another.

You MUST love your neighbor! God's Word says
  it's so.
"And what is a neighbor?" you ask. Soon you'll
  know.
Jesus told what a good neighbor is, and you'll hear
The story that Jesus told—he made it clear.

A smart-aleck lawyer asked Jesus one day,
"Just who is my neighbor? Well, what do you say?"

And Jesus replied to him, quick as a wi**nk**,
"I'll tell you a story. Then see what YOU thi**nk**.

"Tra**mp**, tra**mp**! A Jewish man travels alone.
Then clu**nk** and kerplu**nk**! He grumps and he
  groans.
From in back of a bush, he sees robbers ju**mp**.
They beat him and then his body they du**mp**.
The poor bleeding man soon hollers for he**lp**,
          But the robbers have all run away with
            a ye**lp**!

"Now li**mp** and sore, his body lies still.
Then from way down the road and over the hill,
A priest comes along, but he crosses the street
When he spies the poor man that the
    robbers did beat.

"Sto**mp**, sto**mp**! A church leader
    clo**mps** right on by.
He thi**nks**, 'What a sti**nk**!' and he
    bli**nks** his eye
To forget such a sight. Then he
    sto**mps** away,
For he has more
    important
    business
    today.

"At last a Samaritan man comes along.
He sees the hurt man—knows something is wrong.
He also discovers the man is a Jew.
They are enemies, but he says, 'I will help you!'
Then he lets out a gasp: 'What a bump on your
   head!
You've had quite a thump, and they've left you for
   dead.'

"He patches the lump, gives the hurt man a drink.
Then, willing to risk what his old friends might
   think,
He loads his new friend on his donkey's strong back.
He knows that the man has had quite a bad smack,
So he takes his poor friend to a nearby hotel
And pays for a room where the man can get well.

"That's the end of my story," said Jesus. "Now say
Which guy was the poor hurt man's neighbor that
   day?"

The lawyer was quick—he did not have to thi**nk**.

"Not the priest or the church man," he said with a
   wi**nk**,

"But the one who was kind—the one who gave love.

He's the one who obeyed the Father above."

Words that tickle your tongue
Find these words in the story and say them again: Samaritan,
neighbor, smart aleck, kerplu**nk**, ye**lp**.

Lost and Found: A Story the Good Shepherd Told

Matthew 18:12-14; Luke 15:1-7

Some of the church leaders hea**rd** that Jesus was a frie**nd** to sinners. They came to sco**ld** him for hanging arou**nd** with people who were wi**ld** a**nd** did bad things. It was ha**rd** for them to under-sta**nd** why he would eat with people like that.

So Jesus to**ld** them a story. He wanted to help them have a change of heart that would change their mi**nd**.

*"Suppose that in your ya**rd** you keep*
*A he**rd** of just one hundred*
   sheep.
*A**nd** one small sheep*
   runs from the fold
*A**nd** docs not do as it is to**ld**.*

"Would you not leave the ninety-nine
And go out in the cold to find
That one without a friend or guard
To bring him back into the yard?

"You'd hold him tight, though wild he'd be
And say kind words and help him see
The safest place for growing old
Is in the shepherd's field or fold.

"And then I think, with joyful sound,
You'd tell your neighbors, 'Yay! I've found
My silly sheep that ran away.'
And now, you see, this is the way
That all of heaven rejoices when
One poor lost sinner is found again."

Words that tickle your tongue
Find these words in the story and say them again: herd,
guard.

_t, _k

ct as in act, ft as in left, lt as in belt
nt as in ant, pt as in kept, st as in best,
rt as in part, rk as in work

A Gift and a Feast for a Long-Lost Son

Luke 15:11-32

A man had two sons, and oh, what a pair!
"This young one is making me tear out my hair,"
Said the father. "He's like a young colt, running
  wild.
Why can't he just act like my oldest child?"

The young son did love and respect his father, but he was full of spunk. And he dreamed of a perfect life in the fast-moving city—away from his father's strict rules. He didn't want to think about anyone except himself. So he went to his father and said,

"I'm out of here, Dad! I want to be free.
Please give me the money that's coming to me."
So his gift to each son, the father then gave,
And the wild boy went off to misbehave.

Every cent of his money, he spent in a hurry.
And when it was gone, he began to worry.
He soon had to hunt for food in the street,
While at home, each servant had plenty to eat.
He began to think, "To my dad I will run,
But I'll just be his servant. I can't be his son.
I will say to him, 'Dad, if you'll give me some work,
I will do my best not to act like a jerk.'"

Soon he left the city to go back home. Before he could get to his father's front yard, his dad saw him coming.

Like a bolt of lightning, Dad ran to his boy.
He hugged him and kissed him and shouted with
joy.

To a servant he hollered, "Oh, bring my best
   gown—
And a ring and some sandals—then call the whole
   town
To come for a feast. We will cook a fine roast.
Tell everyone here to prepare
   for the most
SPECTACULAR
   party—no matter
   the cost!
For my son has
   returned—
   the one
   who was
   lost."

About this time, the oldest son was coming in from the fields. He heard the music and dancing. "Just what is going on here?" he asked a servant.

When they told him, he felt he was going to faint.
"My brother? A party? Why, he is no saint!
Why him and not me? I stayed here to work
While he went away, looking back with a smirk."

Then his father ran out to hug him and said,
"I feel like your brother is back from the dead!
I've let go of the hurt I have kept in my heart,
And our family can now make a brand-new start.
I'm so excited to see your young brother.
Rejoice and be glad. Join me and your mother.
My heart is so happy. Oh, son, don't you see?
This party's for everyone—even ME!"

Words that tickle your tongue
Find these words in the story and say them again: colt,
misbehave, bolt of lightning, spectacular, saint.

Jesus and the Children

Matthew 19:13-15; Mark 10:13-16; Luke 18:15-17

*"Hurry, **ch**ildren. This is the day*
The man called Jesus will come our way.
So brush your teeth and comb your hair,
*And **ch**oose a **ch**ange of clothes to*
wear."

All the moms and dads in Galilee wanted their **ch**ildren to meet Jesus. Families got ready early in the morning, packed a lun**ch**, and walked to the place where Jesus was tea**ch**ing. Everyone got quiet when Jesus started talking.

341

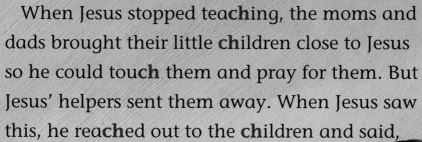

When Jesus stopped teaching, the moms and
dads brought their little **children** close to Jesus
so he could tou**ch** them and pray for them. But
Jesus' helpers sent them away. When Jesus saw
this, he rea**ch**ed out to the **ch**ildren and said,

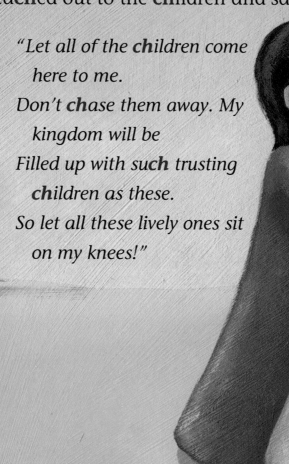

"Let all of the **ch**ildren come
　　here to me.
Don't **ch**ase them away. My
　　kingdom will be
Filled up with su**ch** trusting
　　children as these.
So let all these lively ones sit
　　on my knees!"

Then he held them close to his **ch**est and smiled.
"To my kingdom ea**ch** person must come as a **ch**ild,"
He said as he prayed and hugged ea**ch** **ch**ild tight.
"For when you love God, things are always JUST
    RIGHT!"

Words that tickle your tongue
Find these words in the story and say
them again: **ch**ildren, kingdom.

bl as in **bl**ack, **cl** as in **cl**ose, **fl** as in **fl**y, **gl** as in **gl**ad, **pl** as in **pl**ay, **sl** as in **sl**ow

A Dead Man Clearly Declares God's Glory

John 11:1-45

While Jesus was traveling, he got a message from a **pl**ace called Bethany, where his **cl**ose friends Mary, Martha, and Lazarus lived. The message was short and **cl**ear. It sim**pl**y said:

"Dear Jesus, Our brother, Lazarus, is very— Yes, VERY sick. Love, Martha and Mary."

Jesus read the message, but, oddly, he was **sl**ow to answer. "Lazarus has already died," he told his disciples. "But I am **gl**ad we are not there. Later we will visit Martha and Mary in Bethany, and I will wake Lazarus up from his dead **sl**eep. It will be a good way to show the wonderful **gl**ory of God."

345

The girls loved their brother. Of him they were
  proud.
*But now he was gone, and it seemed a **black cloud**,*
*Like a big heavy **blanket**, hung over their heads.*
*How sad! They just wished they could **climb** in their*
  beds
*And **sleep**—then wake up with a **blink** of their eyes*
*And **fly** to the tomb to see Lazarus rise!*

When Jesus finally got to Bethany, their
dream wish came true. And they didn't even
have to go to **sleep**, for the dream was real! As
Jesus came **close** to town, Martha ran to meet
him.

She said, "If you'd been here, he wouldn't have
  died."
Then they went to the tomb, and Jesus cried.

"Oh, see how this Jesus loved his **close** friend,"
Said the Jews as they watched the Good Master
   bend
Down **close** to the grave. Then they all heard him
   say,
"Your brother will rise. **Clear** the stone away."

Then he prayed to his Father, "Oh, **please** let them
   see
Your wonderful work as you do it through me.
They will know that you sent me. There won't be a
   doubt."
Then he called to his friend, "Oh, Lazarus, come
   out!"

Slowly, so **slowly**, dead Lazarus stood—
As the sisters and Jesus had known that he would—
All wrapped in wide strips of white **cloth** he came,
And he walked toward the Master, who called him
   by name.

*"**P**lease take off the grave **c**lothes and set him free,"*
Said Jesus, his Friend. "Now listen to me:
The people who love me, death CANNOT destroy!"
Then each one who saw this was flooded with joy.
And many who, minutes before, were in grief
*Were **c**lapping and dancing and filled with belief.*
No longer was there any need to be guessing
That Jesus was sent to the earth with God's
   blessing!

Words that tickle your tongue
Find these words in the story and say them again: Bethany,
Lazarus, destroy, grief, belief, blessing.

An Unusual Decision

Luke 19:1-10

A grand occasion was coming up in Jericho.
Jesus was on his way to this busy town.
Everyone wanted to see Jesus. The streets were so
crowded that it looked like there had been a
people explosion!

People standing, people sitting.
People on their knees.
People way up high on rooftops.
People climbing trees.

Climbing trees? Oh, yes!
What is next? You guess!

In all the confusion
there was a small man named
Zaccheus. He was too short to see
over the heads of the taller people
who blocked his vision. So he made a
decision to climb up in a tree to see Jesus.

When Jesus came along that way,
He looked up in that tree.
"Zaccheus, come on down," he said.
"And go to your house with me."

"It will be my pleasure to take you there," said Zaccheus. But the people who were watching were surprised that Jesus would go home with a man like Zach. He was a tax collector, and tax collectors usually were not honest people.

Zach just smiled, but
  others muttered.
They didn't think it funny.
Their conclusion was that
  Zach
Stole other people's money.
So why would Jesus do this
  thing?
Why go to be the guest
Of one who was a well-known
  crook
When he could visit the best?

Then Zach spoke up. He
  said, "It's true—
I have a lot of treasure,

But if I've cheated anyone,
I'll pay them, for good measure,
FOUR times what I owe them. Now,
  Would anyone do more?
  And half of everything that's mine,
    I'll give to feed the poor."

Then Jesus said, "Now listen up!
Zaccheus is a winner—
  For I have come to find and save
  All those like this rich sinner!"

  Then Zach and Jesus went off
  together to Zach's house.

Words that tickle your tongue
Find these words in the story and say them again:
occasion, explosion, confusion, Zaccheus, pleasure,
tax collector, conclusion, treasure, measure.

chr as in Christ, phr as in phrase,
shr as in shrub, spr as in spring,
str as in strong, thr as in three

A Strange Parade
of Three

Matthew 21:1-9; Mark 11:1-10; Luke 19:28-38; John 12:12-15

It was **spr**ingtime—time for Passover. Everyone was traveling to Jerusalem to celebrate. On the way there, Jesus and his disciples were **str**olling **thr**ough a small village. "**Spr**int on ahead," Jesus said to two of his friends. "Go **str**aight until you see a donkey tied up with her **spr**y little colt. Untie them and bring them to me."

"If anyone sees you and tells you to stop
Or thinks you are stealing and calls for a cop,
Just tell him the Lord needs the donkeys today,
And he'll gladly send them with you right away."

The two disciples **spr**ang into action and found the animals exactly where Jesus had said they would be. The disciples brought the donkey and her colt **str**aight back to Jesus. Then the men **thr**ew their coats on the young donkey's back so Jesus could ride it.

Great **thr**ongs of people **str**eamed
through the **str**eet,
But when they saw Jesus, they fell at his
feet.
Some of them **spr**ead their
coats on the ground,
And others laid palm-leaf
sprigs all around
On his path, or they
stretched to wave
them up high
To celebrate Jesus as he
rode by.

The **strong** little donkey carried him
   through
The crowds. And everyone
   struggled to view
His face. In **shr**ill voices, they shouted
   the **phr**ase,
"Hosanna, praise God!" and many
   threw sprays
Of their branches and leaves. They were SO
   thrilled to see
This **str**anger. But some of them asked,
   "Who is he?"
"It's the prophet from Nazareth in Galilee,"
Cried the crowds in the **str**eet. "Oh, blessed is he!"

A parade of **thr**ee—how **str**ange! Just one
man and two donkeys. Jesus rode
through the **str**eets of Jerusalem while
throngs of people **str**etched their necks
to see him.

"Hosanna to the Son of David!" cried the crowd. "Blessed is he who comes in the name of the Lord."

Many people were just beginning to understand that Jesus was the **Chr**ist— the Bethlehem baby who was born to be a king.

Words that tickle your tongue
Find these words in the story and say them again: **str**olling, **spr**y, **str**eamed, **spr**igs, **str**etched, **str**uggled, Hosanna.

Food, Truth, and Sad News at the Last Supper Together with Jesus

Matthew 26:17-30; Mark 14:12-26; Luke 22:1-23

Jesus was planning to eat a special Passover supper with his disciples. He told Peter and John where to find a dining **roo**m and how to prepare the f**oo**d. The disciples were in a happy m**oo**d as they sat and rested on their benches and st**oo**ls around the big table. They were ready to enjoy the Passover feast together with their leader.

While they were eating, Jesus told them some sad news:

"Very soon the time will come
When I must go away,
And I must share with you some truth
That's hard for me to say.
For one of you now sitting here
Is not a faithful friend.

"Instead, he is my enemy—
A fake—he just pretends
To love me. But he's made a deal—
Already he's agreed—
He'll give me to some foolish men
Who plan an evil deed."

The **moo**d of the men in the **room** was suddenly gl**oo**my. Was one of them really crude and cruel enough to do such a horrible thing? Several disciples began to ask Jesus if they could be the one. With a smirk on his face, Judas Iscariot asked rudely, "I am not the one, am I?"

Jesus said to him,

*"Judas, do not **foo**l with me!*
Pretending isn't funny.
Already you have traded me
For lots of silver money."

Then Jesus picked up some bread. He gave thanks. He broke it into pieces and gave it to the disciples and said, "You will eat together like this many times. Each time you break the bread, let it remind you of my body, which will be broken for you."

Then he offered them a cup of wine, saying,

"Now every time you drink from this cup,
Remember the life that I will give up,
And the blood that will flow so that God can forgive
The sins of the world and all people may live."

All the disciples in the **room** heard this truth, and they knew that the time for Jesus to die was near. So the whole group sang together one of their favorite tunes—a hymn. Then they went to a quiet garden where Jesus could pray.

Words that tickle your tongue
Find these words in the story and say them again: crude, cruel, rudely.

More phonics fun
Read this story again to find every **o** that sounds like the **o** in t**o**, every **ew** that sounds like the **ew** in n**ew**, and every **u** that sounds like the **u** in J**u**ne.

A Sad Good-bye for Those Who Stood by a Wooden Cross

Matthew 26:47-50, 27:11-54; Mark 14:43-65, 15:1-39;
Luke 22:47, 23:1-47; John 18:1-5, 19:1-30

Jesus had been in a garden talking to his Father in heaven for a long time. In the middle of the night, as he stood in the garden with his disciples, he looked up to see Judas Iscariot coming toward him. Jesus knew there was no time left to say good-bye to his friends. Behind Judas he could see a large crowd of men with swords and clubs. As they came closer, Judas said to the crowd,

371

"The man I will kiss—it is he who's the one."
Then he ran to kiss Jesus. The evil was done!

The angry crowd grabbed Jesus. Pushing and pulling and making fun of him, they took him to Pilate, the Roman governor. "This man is up to no good," they said. "Kill him!"

The disciples were afraid and ran away. They pretended they did not know Jesus.

When Pilate saw Jesus, he said to the angry people,

"What IS this man's crime? What terrible thing
Has he done?" (They answered, "He says he's a
    king!")
Then Pilate asked Jesus, "Good man, if you would,
Please tell me if you are a king." Jesus stood.

"I was born to be king. And I came to forgive
The sins of the world so that all can live."

Pilate could think of no good reason to kill Jesus, so he asked the crowd to let Jesus go.

But the crowd believed that Jesus was a fake—a crook—so they shook their fists and gave him dirty looks. "Crucify him! Crucify him!" they cried.

"He's a liar. He says that he is God's Son."
Pilate wanted to stop them, but they had won.
This mob wanted Jesus. They wanted him dead.
So the soldiers crowned him with thorns on his head.

And they made him carry a cross of wood

To a place where two other crosses stood

On an ugly hill, and they hung him high

As they laughed and mocked him and watched
him die.

Then the light of the sun the dark did erase.

Even God could not look at his dying Son's face.

When Jesus cried out, "It is finished, it's done,"

A soldier who heard thought, "This must be
God's Son!"

And everyone watching had fear in his heart,

For the earth shook so hard that huge rocks
split apart.

Now even the guards would know it was true

That the man they had killed was the very one who

Was born on this earth to be king of the Jews.

It was time to believe the truth of this news!

Words that tickle your tongue
Find these words in the story and say them again:
Pilate, crook, crucify.

More phonics fun
Read this story again to find every **u** that sounds like the **u** in bush and every **ou** that sounds like the **ou** in could.

The Amazing, Hair-raising Resurrection Story

Matthew 27:62–28:10; Mark 16:1-8; Luke 24:1-10

This is the story of Easter. It is not about bunnies or baskets of colored eggs or flowers. It is about something much more important and exciting. It is about God's power to make dead things come alive again.

Jesus of Nazareth had been dead three days.
No smiles, no cheers, no glad hoorays
Were heard. His friends were quiet and sad.
The men who hated Jesus had
A meeting. They all remembered when
Jesus had said, "I will rise again!"

379

Outside of the
  tomb where
  Jesus lay,
A huge stone
  blocked the
  small doorway.
The men were
  worried—they
  were afraid
Because of the
  promise Jesus
  had made.
What if this man
  from the cross
  should survive?
What if he WAS
  once again
  alive?

Some guards should
    be sent to stand
    nearby
To watch just in case
    Jesus' friends
    should try
To sneak around in
    the dark of night
And come to that
    tomb so safe and
    tight
And roll that oversize
    stone away
And steal Jesus' body.
    Then they would
    say
That their Jesus now
    lives—just as he
    said.
How silly—NObody
    gets up from the
    dead!

Nobody (not even the disciples) believed for sure that Jesus would be resurrected—that he would come back to life. Yes, they all remembered that Jesus had said, "All power is mine in heaven and earth." They heard him say it, but they just did NOT get it!

Silly people.
Silly men.
Silly guards.
Silly friends.

What a surprise was waiting for all of them.

On Sunday morning, the earth did quake.
The guards began to shiver and shake.
Then suddenly, down from the skies—KABOOM!
Two angels appeared in front of the tomb.
The one pushed away the stone with his shoulder,
And then he sat down on that oversize boulder.

Some ladies who came to see Jesus were near,
And the angel surprised them: "He is not here!
Please tell all his friends that he is alive."
And before that angel could count to five,
Those ladies, as if they had wings on their shoes,
Ran off to share the hair-raising news
That Jesus had risen—just as he said.
"He's alive! Yes, Jesus is back from
   the dead!"

Words that tickle your tongue
Find these words in the story and say them again: amazing,
hair-raising, resurrection, Easter, oversize, KABOOM.

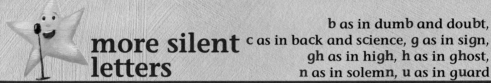

more silent letters

b as in dumb and doubt,
c as in back and science, g as in sign,
gh as in high, h as in ghost,
n as in solemn, u as in guard

Doubting Disciples Believe They See a Ghost

Mark 16:12-19; Luke 24:13-51; John 20:19-21; Acts 1:2-9

Jesus had folded his grave clothes and climbed out of the tomb, ALIVE! The angel had sent some women to run quickly from the scene to tell his disciples, but NO one would believe them. The doubters just chuckled and said,

"These women are wacky—they are sick in the head.
They think that Jesus is back from the dead!"

On that same day, the real, live Jesus saw two of his friends out walking. As he caught up with them, he heard them talking about him, but they did not know who he was.

387

Just for fun, he asked them a tricky question:

"What are you saying? Tell me what's new."
They looked dumbfounded and said, "Are you
A visitor? Did you just now arrive?
Some women have heard that Christ is alive!"
He listened to them as they told the story—
Even the parts that were gross and gory.
And then they invited him home to eat.
But when he broke bread, they turned white as a
    sheet,
For they knew they were eating with Jesus—how
    weird!
Then quick as a wink, Jesus disappeared!

Later that day the disciples were hiding
together in a locked room. They were numb
with fear. They were afraid of the Jewish
leaders. The guards might have lied and said
the disciples stole Jesus' body from the grave.

The disciples were nearly sick with gloom
When suddenly, Jesus appeared in the room!

How ghastly! So frightened were they that most
Of them thought for sure they were seeing a ghost!
Then Jesus said, "Peace! Oh, why do you doubt?
And why look so solemn and all stressed out?"

They thought they were seeing a ghost, but he
Just held out his hands—"Come, touch and see."
And there was a change in their attitude
When he said, "Hey, I'm hungry! Got
   any food?"

The disciples were so flabbergasted they could hardly move, but they needed no more signs that Jesus was alive. Right away, they brought him some fish to eat. When he picked up the fish with his thumbs and fingers and ate it, they knew for sure that he was real.

For at least forty more days and nights, Jesus and these men whom he had picked to be his best friends enjoyed being together. He taught them about the kingdom of God, and he gave them their assignment—things they should do after he was gone.

Then one day he called them to say good-bye,
And they all gathered 'round him, for now they
   knew why
He was leaving. And all of them knew what to do.
He had told them, "My power will come to you
By the Holy Spirit, and you will share
My message with all people—EVERYWHERE."

After he said this, he was taken up through a
cloud into the sky.

Words that tickle your tongue
Find these words in the story and say them again: doubting,
ghost, chuckled, wacky, dumbfounded, ghastly, solemn,
flabbergasted, assignment.

_l, _r, s_

On page 400 is a complete
list of the featured sounds
reviewed in this story.

Jesus' Brave Friends Start Spreading the Good News

Acts 1–5

When Jesus was taken up into heaven, he left a small group of friends with a job to do. But first they had to choose another disciple to take the place of Judas—the one who had not been a true friend to Jesus. There were just eleven special disciples left.

"We need a new man on our team," they said.
"One who will gladly help us spread
The news, as we have been asked to do.
We have a short list of names—just two!"
Then they prayed and asked God, "Which one of
these men
Is the one we should choose? Please show us.
Amen!"

Then God helped them know that Matthias was the right choice to be disciple number twelve.

When the Jewish holiday called Pentecost came, all twelve of the men plus many others were together in a house.

*SWOOSH! Like the wings of a **great**, **swift** bird*
*Or the **blast** of a **blizzard** was the sound that was*
*   heard.*
*And it came **from** heaven and filled the **place**.*
Just imagine the look on everyone's face—
*Perhaps they all **blinked** or **broke** out in hives,*
Grabbed on to each other and feared for their lives!
Did they quake? Did they shake? Did they all run
*   away?*
*Oh, no! They did not even **cry** out—or **pray**—*
For they weren't surprised. They knew Jesus would
*   send*
*His **Spirit** to rest upon each special friend.*

*They did not think the **Sp**irit would be quite so loud,*
*But they **stayed close***
  together and sat
  *__st__ill and **pr**oud.*
*They **tru**ly believed that*
  this was the hour
*That God's Holy **Sp**irit would*
  fill them with power.

And that's exactly what happened. Jesus had kept his **pr**omise. And now, with God's power, they were **pr**epared to do the work that John the Baptist and Jesus had **st**arted. Jesus' disciples baptized new believers, healed sick and **br**oken bodies, and did many other miracles.

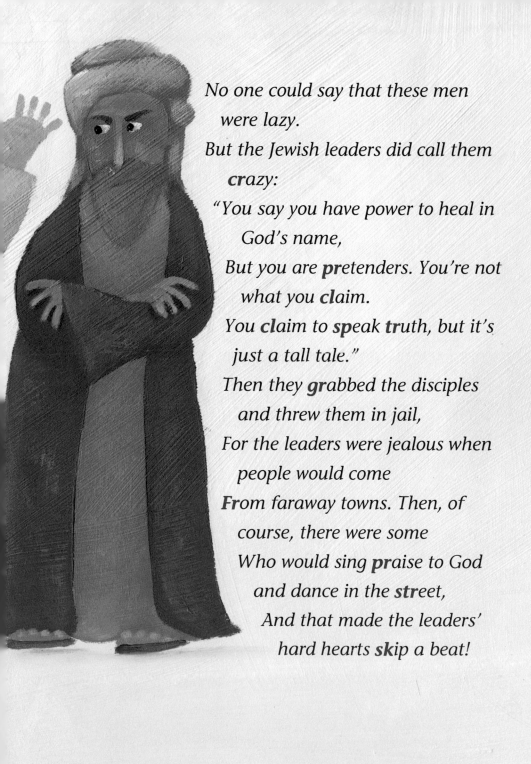

No one could say that these men
were lazy.
But the Jewish leaders did call them
crazy:
"You say you have power to heal in
God's name,
But you are **pr**etenders. You're not
what you **cl**aim.
You **cl**aim to **sp**eak **tr**uth, but it's
just a tall tale."
Then they **gr**abbed the disciples
and threw them in jail,
For the leaders were jealous when
people would come
From faraway towns. Then, of
course, there were some
Who would sing **pr**aise to God
and dance in the **str**eet,
And that made the leaders'
hard hearts **sk**ip a beat!

They **sl**ammed the door of the jail **and** locked it up tight. How **sc**ary! "That will **st**op you **cr**azy followers of Jesus **from fl**ying around, **st**irring up **tr**ouble, and telling your **st**upid **st**ories," they thought.

But the **gr**umpy leaders were about to see something that would make their bulging eyeballs **br**eak out of their sockets and **dr**op into their pockets!

During the night, an angel of the Lord opened the **str**ong, locked **pr**ison door so the disciples could **sn**eak out. When those **gr**ouchy leaders got up in the morning, they saw the disciples **st**anding in **fr**ont of the temple, telling people about God.

From town to town and house to house, the disciples **tr**aveled. They never **st**opped telling the **gr**eat news about God's love!

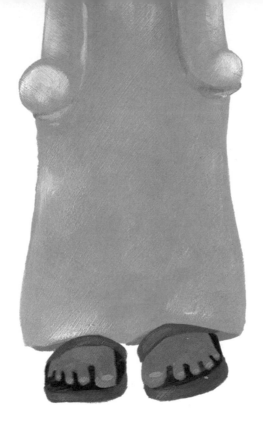

(Hey, do you suppose those **sp**unky leaders ever got their eyeballs out of their pockets?)

Review of sounds
This story reviews these beginning blends:
l blends—**bl, cl, fl, gl, pl, sl**
r blends—**br, cr, dr, fr, gr, pr, tr**
s blends—**sc, sk, sl, sm, sn, sp, spr, st, str, sw**

Words that tickle your tongue
Find these words in the story and say them again: Matthias, Pentecost, **SW**OOSH, **bl**izzard, imagine, **pr**etenders, bulging eyeballs, sockets, **sp**unky.

ch, gh, ng, sh, th, wh

On page 407 is a complete list of the featured sounds reviewed in this story.

An Angry Man with a Rough Reputation Is Chosen by God

Acts 9

Everybody knew about Saul. He had a reputation! He was a hater. He hated Jesus. He hated the disciples. And he hated the **church**—anyone who loved Jesus.

Oh, my, he was rough!
He could not do enough
To hurt God's people
And make their lives tough.

His bad reputation
Never took a vacation!

From house to house he went to search
For the men and women who were part of God's
   church.
He would chase them and catch them and lock
   them in chains.
Just thinking of Christians would make him insane.

But Saul's angry actions were not enough to stop that busy bunch of disciples. They went right on cheerfully teaching and preaching and reaching out to touch each sick person who wished to be healed. Angry Saul kept doing everything he could think of to shut them up, but they paid no attention.

Suddenly someone got Saul's attention.

He was walking along the road to a city called Damascus, where he hoped to find more men and women who belonged to God's church so he could put them in jail.

But just outside of the city—

Shock of all shocks—a strong light from the sky
Started shining on him, and a voice called out,
  "Why
Do you pick on my people and mess with ME?"
Saul tried to look up, but he could not see.

His eyes were blind. He asked, "Lord, who are you?"
And the voice said, "I'm Jesus. Get up and do
What I tell you. Go into the city and find
A man who will help you, since now you are blind."

Then God chose a man whom he called in a dream.
"Ananias," he said, "I need YOU on my team!
Now go to a house and ask to see Saul."
Ananias didn't like this assignment at all.
"But Lord, Saul is out to destroy us. He's mad!
And his reputation is frightfully bad!"

But, strange as it seemed, Saul was the one God had chosen to take his message to many people. God helped Ananias understand that. So the man went to meet Saul.

Ananias touched Saul's eyes and said, "The Lord Jesus, who showed his shining power to you on the road, has sent me so that you may see again and be filled with the Holy Spirit."

*How astoni**sh**ing!*
*What a **ch**ange!*
*God **ch**ose a **church**-hater.*
Isn't that strange?

*Saul's **ch**ance of surivi**ng***
Seemed terribly slim,
For now the bad guys
*Would **ch**ase after him!*

But Saul was **th**ankful to be on God's team.
He went right to work, prea**ching** and tea**ching**
that Jesus is the Son of God.

Review of sounds
This story reviews these groups of letters that form new
sounds: **ch** as in **ch**urch, **gh** as in lau**gh**, **ng** as in stro**ng**,
sh as in **sh**ine, **th** as in **th**ank, **wh** as in **wh**ite.

Words that tickle your tongue
Find these words in the story and say them again:
reputation, Damascus, Ananias, surivi**ng**.

More phonics fun
Read this story again to find every **t** that sounds
like the **t** in nation.

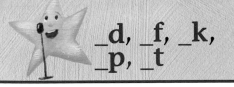

_d, _f, _k,
_p, _t

On page 413 is a complete list of the featured sounds reviewed in this story.

Bold Prisoners Help a Frightened Guard Become a Friend of God

Acts 16:16-34

Saul, the man who met Jesus on the road to Damascus, changed his name to Paul. Each day he and his new friend, Silas, held meetings where they told the story of Jesus to many people. They worked hard to help people understand how much Jesus loved them.

One day some men got angry with Paul and Silas for saving a girl from an evil spirit. They grabbed the two friends and dragged them to the front of the police station. They asked the police to lock Paul and Silas up:

409

"These two men you cannot trust,
For they make trouble. So you must
Put them in jail and bolt them down,
Or they will surely spoil our town."

The friends were beaten then were swept
Away to jail, where they were kept
Inside a room as dark as night—
No windows there to let in light.
Their hands and wrists were tied with cords.
Their feet were bound with chains to boards.
And to the guard, these words were said:
"If you let these guys get away, you're dead!"

Wow! Those angry men did NOT mess around. They meant what they said. But Paul and Silas were not worried:

They did not grump. They did not slump—
Didn't let their spirits get down in a dump.
Instead, the other prisoners heard
The brave, bold men sing every word
Of all the happy hymns they knew.
And they prayed aloud to You Know Who!

At midnight, without any warning, something very strange happened.

The ground began to shift and shake,
And the floor of the jail began to break.
Great chunks of wall fell into the street,
And the chains shook loose from the
    prisoners' feet.

While this jumbling and jolting twisted the
    place,
Gasping and gulping, the jailer's face
    Appeared in the dark. And he
      stumbled toward
      The prisoners as he lifted his
        sword
      To take his own life. But Paul yelled
        in his ear,
    "Please DON'T hurt yourself, for we
      are all here!"

The jailer knelt down on the broken sod:
"What must I do to know your God?"

"Believe in the Lord Jesus Christ!" he was told.
"And then your whole family—young and old—
Will be saved. It is simple. That's all you must do.
Just believe in your heart Jesus died for you."

The jailer lifted his head to thank Paul and Silas, and he was kind enough to take them home and wash their wounds. Right away, he and his family were baptized. Then he invited his new friends to breakfast.

As they ate and drank together, he told everyone how joyful he felt because now he and his family believed in Jesus.

Review of sounds
This story reviews these ending blends:
ld, nd, rd, lf, nk, rk, sk, lp, mp, sp, ct, ft, lt, nt, pt, rt, st.

Words that tickle your tongue
Find these words in the story and say them again:
police station, slump, shift, chunks,
jumbling, jolting, twisted, wounds.

413

The Best "Happily Ever After" Ever!

Revelation 21

This story has the best ending of any story in the world. That's because it is God's story, and he ends it just as he begins it—full of light, full of joy, and full of surprises!

In the beginning, the surprises were these:
A sun and a moon and fruits and trees.
At the end, the surprises are streets of gold
With gates of pearl and jewels to behold—
A city that needs no sun for its light
And no moon because it is NEVER night!
The city is full of the light of God's glory,
And its lamp is Jesus. Oh, what a great story!

Imagine a place that
 twinkles with light,
A perfect city with
 everything right—
Where nothing is bad or
 mad or sad,
But only good and loving
 and glad.

No dirt, no messes, no need for a broom,
And there no one ever says, "Clean up your room!"
No ugly words like quarrel *and* grouch
Or rude *and* cruel *and* hurt *and* ouch.
No greed or anger or anything rotten.
In heaven, all evil will be forgotten!

No scars, no scabs, no itches to scratch,
No sores, no bruises, no colds to catch.
And no one is dumb—there is never a test,
'Cuz there, every student can be the best.

Nothing is broken, and no one is lame,
And there's never a need to take the
    blame
For things that are wrong. There are no
   mistakes,
  No liars, no cheaters, no thieves, no fakes.

No fighting or argument ever begins,
So there are no losers—EVERYONE wins!
And there's nothing at all to make you afraid,
For all things in heaven are things that God made.
No one who lives there gets sick or cries.
No one grows old, and no one dies.

No crying? No dying? Can this be true?
Yes! "Look," says God. "I make everything NEW!

"So come to my home, and stay here forever,
Where singing, rejoicing, and laughing together
Never will stop." He invites you to come—
Whoever you are and wherever you're from.

Fire-truck drivers and doctors and queens,
Parents and children and kids in their teens
Will hold hands with prophets, disciples, and
    preachers—
A jubilant gathering of God's human creatures!

How amazing! How astonishing! It's simply stupendous! Isn't it almost too thrilling to think about? YOU are invited to live with God, your heavenly Father. He wants the pleasure of sharing his home with you—just because he loves you.

Now you and all God's people can say yes to his invitation and live together HAPPILY EVER AFTER!

Words that tickle your tongue
Find these words in the story and say them again: pearl, jewels, jubilant gathering, invitation.

More phonics fun
On the next page is a list of the 44 sounds in the English language. Listen for each sound in this story. (You won't have colored letters to help you because every word is a different combination of these 44 sounds.)

the end

The 44 Sounds of the English Language

VOWEL SOUNDS

Short Vowel Sounds
1. a (cap)
2. e (bed)
3. i (fish)
4. o (pop)
5. u (cup, son)

Long Vowel Sounds
6. a (lake, pray, main, they, yea)
7. e (feet, eat, people, believe, baby)
8. i (kite, night, cry, buy)
9. o (go, home, low)
10. u [yoo] (mule, few)

More Vowel Sounds
11. uh (asleep, Jonathan, Israel, Goliath)
12. air (care, hair, scary, bear, their, very)
13. er (her, bird, worry, curl)
14. ah (father, jar)
15. aw (ball, saw, talk, cross)
16. oi (oil, boy)
17. ou (house, down)
18. oo (moon, to, new, June)
19. oo (book, bush, could)

CONSONANT SOUNDS

Single Letters
20. b (boat)
21. d (dog)
22. f (fox, alphabet, laugh)
23. g (gate)

24. h (hat)
25. j (Jericho, giant, page, judge)
26. k (cat, king, back)
27. l (lamp)
28. m (mop)
29. n (nest)
30. p (pig)
31. r (rat, write)
32. s (sun, face)
33. t (ten)
34. v (vase)
35. w (water)
36. y (yarn)
37. z (zebra, nose)

Digraphs
(Two letters that make one new sound)

38. ch (chair, lunch)
39. sh (shark, fish, nation)
40. zh (treasure, vision)
41. th (thank, teeth)
42. th (the, together)
43. wh (hw) (wheel)
44. ng (king)

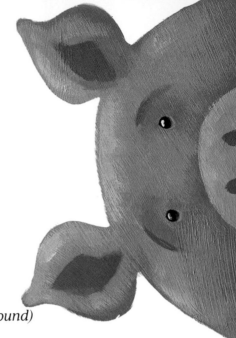

These are the sounds of our language that are addressed by all systems of phonetic instruction. Practice in recognizing letter combinations that stand for these sounds will empower young learners in their quest to become good readers.

Blends and clusters: Several letters can be combined to form a variety of beginning and ending consonant blends and clusters. However, these combinations create no new sounds. There is simply a blend of two or three of the forty-four sounds.

Silent letters: Some words contain letters that are silent. Of course, silent letters can't create a new sound either! So the total number of sounds stays at forty-four.

JOY MACKENZIE, the oldest daughter of a preacher-dad and a teacher-mom, grew up in a loving home where supper was served with Scripture and Shakespeare. As a result, she developed a love for God and people as well as a lifelong romance with words and teaching.

"Perhaps," says Joy, "though I grew older, I never really grew up, for I am still as delighted and intrigued with the Bible stories of my childhood as when they were first read to me. What fun it has been to revisit them as an adult who still hears and sees from the perspective of a child."

Joy's continuing enthusiasm for kid stuff is evident in her professional life, which has included teaching every elementary and high school grade (working with both gifted and academically challenged students), six years of teaching at the college level, nationwide tours as an educational consultant, twenty years as vice president of an educational publishing company, and authoring more than fifty books. Her published works include many resources for teachers and dozens of religious books and recordings for children and their families.

As chairman of the English department at Nashville's Christ Presbyterian Academy, this lover of literature and life divides her time between teaching, writing, speaking, consulting, and being "Mom" to two grown daughters.

JILL NEWTON was born in Newcastle, England (in the northeast part of the country). She grew up in Lincoln, where she learned to ride and fall off bicycles and horses and did a lot of other fun stuff when she was at school.

Jill studied art at Lincoln Art College and illustration at Cambridge College of Art. She explains that Cambridge was very cold, so when she finished her studies she moved to London (Hackney), where she stayed for fourteen years. She claims that this is quite an achievement by most people's standards.

A nature lover and friend of animals, Jill now lives in a small village in Somerset with her good horse, Samuel, who has been with her since he gave up racing a number of years ago. Jill says her horse tells her he has no intention of returning. (Jill has told Sam not to worry. She doesn't think he is going to be asked back.) Benjamin, the sheep puppy, has come to stay too. He and Jill go out exploring together.

Jill has been illustrating children's books since she left college. She has also worked in advertising, design, and TV. In addition to that, she had a brief escapade as a bicycle courier, delivering a variety of packages to their destination.